IRISH
COUNTRY STYLE

IRISH
COUNTRY STYLE

BILL LAWS

AURUM

First published in Great Britain
1999 by Aurum Press Ltd
25 Bedford Avenue, London WC1B 3AT

Design by Roger Daniels

Picture research by Gabrielle Allen

A catalogue record for this book is available from the British Library.

ISBN 1 85410 523 X

10 9 8 7 6 5 4 3 2 1
2003 2002 2001 2000 1999

Printed in Singapore by C.S. Graphics

Contents

ACKNOWLEDGEMENTS

The author owes a debt of gratitude to all those Irish people who welcomed him into their homes and to the assistance of Bord Fáilte, Annie Bowyer in County Galway, Roger Callow, Chelsey Fox, Dr Alan Gailey of the Ulster Folk and Transport Museum, basket-maker Sandy Green, the Irish Trade Board, Michael Kenny, Thornton Kay and Hazel Maltravers of SALVO, Terry Lynch, Marcus Patton and Hearth, Jerry Ross, Jonathan Seddon-Harvey, Viv Southorn, the late Mary Redden and, finally, Abby Laws for her patient support.

Bill Laws travelled in Ireland with CIE Tours.

> *'I've heard people, including the Irish,*
> *ask if there ever was such a thing as an Irish*
> *country style. In a country as rich as ours*
> *in landscape, language, character and culture,*
> *how could they ever doubt it?'*

Introduction

OPPOSITE PAGE

Irish country homes are pretty, but practical. Features such as these flagstone floors, simple wood and rush seats, traditional lamps and picture frames and even the old cooking crane over the turf fire still survive to this day. They are a precious resource and a link with the past.

FIRST IMPRESSIONS OF IRISH COUNTRY STYLE suggest a genteel disorder and an anything-goes approach that defies convention. This free-flowing fusion of eclectic interiors and traditional exteriors, of confident colours and mix-and-match materials has its origins in the folk arts and cottage crafts of Ireland. It does not conform to any preconceptions of chintzy chic or floral print; nor is it waiting to be collected, ready-made, from the shelves of a designer store. Rooted in the rural economies of the nineteenth century, it has been adopted by resourceful and imaginative homemakers and successfully brought in to complement the modern house and its garden.

The making of this book provoked lively debates on the whole idea of Irish country style in places as diverse as a comfortably chaotic Galway farmhouse and a bar in County Kerry which, apart from a bare electric light bulb hanging from the ceiling, had not seen the need to change its looks in sixty years. On one of these occasions a visiting American interior designer suggested that if only the people would 'forget their browns' the Irish look could become as renowned as French or Scandinavian style. On another occasion, a blow-in from London thought that Irish country style might have existed some time before the invasion of the bungalow, but was now long lost and forgotten. Both comments aroused a spirited defence of Irish heritage from the others present. The most eloquent reply came from a young

Irish art student who was studying the potter's craft. 'I've heard people, including the Irish, ask if there ever was such a thing as an Irish country style. In a country as rich as ours in landscape, language, character and culture, how could they ever doubt it?' she wanted to know.

Different people have different ideas about what constitutes true Irish country style. The proud possessors of an old farmhouse in County Sligo might see it in the harmonious way that their sharp, bright stone walls stand out against the deep greenery of the garden. For their friends in Cork, it is crisp Irish bedlinen, a Celtic knotwork stencil and a collection of handmade lace samplers which seem to embody the spirit of the style. Meanwhile, in a carefully restored cottage in Munster, Irish country style is suggested by the faded fabric of a red-and-white Ulster patchwork quilt displayed against the distressed distemper of rough plastered walls.

The common thread running through these scenes, and through the inspiring photographs that follow, is the elemental Irishness of it all. From the shape of a shamrock to the design of a wickerwork peat basket, there is no mistaking the Irish touch.

This book celebrates the seductive charms of the Irish country style, from homespun County Donegal in the north to the fashionable interiors of County Cork in the south. It provides a timely reminder of the traditional elements of Irish style – whether it is the vernacular designs of the homes of the provinces, or the distinctive characteristics of country furniture. And it gives an insight into the inspirational way in which these elements fit into a contemporary setting, from the glow of a peat fire caught in the cut of Irish crystal glass to clusters of herbs hanging to dry from an old, varnished hatstand in a kitchen.

LEFT

*C*ountry styles are a compromise between custom and convenience, originating from a time when thrift and economy were the order of the day. Despite similarities, every country style has its distinctive differences. This nineteenth-century interior illustrates some sensible conventions: the kitchen table stands beneath a well-lit window, salt is stored in a dry box beside the hearth, a small spy-hole window in the wall throws light where needed.

THE PAST

Country styles are rooted in rural history. Whether it is the whitewashed wood of the Scandinavian farmhouse, the terracotta tiles of Tuscany, or Windsor chairs in an English country kitchen, the essential ingredients of any country style can be traced back to the industriousness and ingenuity of rural people who were restricted to working with natural materials such as wood, rush, reed and clay.

Before cheap, mass-produced materials spelled the end of the vernacular tradition, simple solutions born out of prudence and economy lay at the heart of the typical Irish home: painted wooden chairs drawn up around a scrubbed-top, pine table; a brass bedstead covered in a colourful quilt constructed from off-cuts and scraps of cloth; a high-backed settle made from salvaged packing case timbers; space-saving fold-down beds and drop-down tables; a bow-legged turf-burning stove, which cooked the meals and warmed the home.

The country homes themselves, built as they were from the local earth, stone and more rarely the wood of the neighbourhood, were purposeful buildings specifically designed to serve the particular needs of their inhabitants. Their use of natural fabrics, their proportions – one storey high and one room deep – and their position – nestling down among the Irish greenery – made them appear as natural in the landscape as the buttercups in a meadow. The poet William Wordsworth described the dark slate houses of his native Cumbria as seeming to have risen 'by an instinct of their own, out of the native rock, so little is there in them of formality, such is their wildness and beauty'. He could have said the same about the blackstone villages of County Down or some low-browed, whitewashed longhouse tucked in under a sheltering hill beside the coast of Connemara.

The vernacular (the word comes from a Latin root meaning a slave born in his master's house and therefore a homegrown native) was a local affair which changed from one county to another and even from one parish to another. Although no two of these handmade houses were identical, they shared enough common characteristics to give a particular flavour to each neighbourhood. Ireland is the most westerly outpost of Europe and village life could be isolated and remote. People built their homes to the same designs, and cultivated their gardens by the same methods, as the rest of their community because, often, this was all they knew and trusted. Country people, however, were not nostalgic sentimentalists who aspired to the simple life. They were no less houseproud nor hungry for change than their more affluent and worldly neighbours, and if the old thatch leaked and an affordable alternative such as slate could be had at a decent price, the thatch would go, no matter how picturesque.

As new ideas, new technologies and new materials reached across Ireland, the distinctive vernacular styles inevitably began to slip away. The pace of change was accelerated when, in the early nineteenth century, every country gentleman seemed to be building for himself one of those solid, square Georgian villas which still stand scattered across rural Ireland. The influence of these fashionable out-of-town residences soon filtered down the social scale. They impressed the artisans and the craftsmen, and persuaded them that they too should part with seven hundred guineas and build for themselves a modest villa or hunting lodge, if they turned a little profit and enjoyed a good year.

Setting aside its long and sometimes troubled history, Ireland's past was forged by these same artisans and craftspeople, and this remains a country in which the craft of local distinctiveness has been developed into an art. Take the men of the Ulster spade mills who, a century ago, worked to meet the specific demands of local soils and local traditions. The spade makers, their skills passed on from generation to generation, manufactured more than one hundred different styles of spade from the thin, bladed 'loys' of the south and west to the two-shouldered Ulster digging spade. (Anyone coming across an old spade in his or her garden shed today should treat it with respect, since it may have become a collector's item.) The spinner and saddler, the carpenter and candle maker, the basket maker and blacksmith all fashioned their functional but fine objects from local materials and for local markets. With such an inheritance, it is no wonder that Irish householders still retain a distinct preference for their own country's lace, linen, weavings, quilts, china and glass.

Irish country style harks back to the days when the household hens roosted overnight on the bottom shelf of the kitchen dresser and when, during festivities, the back door of the house would be taken down and used as a resonant, temporary dance floor. Those days may be long gone and yet the past sometimes survives in the present: the painted dresser still holds court in many a country kitchen, for example, and the back door, safely restored to its hinges, opens out on to cottage-style gardens flourishing under an agreeable climate.

These same small country gardens were once filled with plants grown for their medicinal, culinary and superstitious qualities: lavender, which was reputed to keep fleas at bay, and a red rowan tree, grown to ward away witchcraft, would share their growing space with the cottagers' soaring hollyhocks and scented roses. As with Ireland's vernacular buildings, the character of these country gardens changed from one area to another and a rocky, weatherworn plot clinging to the shores of the Atlantic in County Mayo painted a very different picture to some hothouse garden of exotics languishing near the warming waters of the gulf stream in County Kerry. Like the vernacular houses, these practical and productive gardens gradually fell under the spell of the grand gardens that surrounded the homes of the wealthy. Thanks to the discreet trade in seeds, seedlings and cuttings between the gardeners who worked at the grand houses and their village neighbours, cottage gardens enjoyed a steady supply of new plants and species. And the idea of features such as trelliswork dividers, hung with creeping honeysuckle, or kitchen gardens, hedged around with

BELOW

*G*rand gardens were conceived as fashion accessories, but the burgeoning cottage garden was as productive as it was pleasant. Hidden among the casual arrangements of poppies, tulips and wallflowers in this little Wicklow garden are plants grown for their medicinal, culinary and even ritual purposes.

privet, were similarly borrowed from the grand gardens, scaled down and integrated into the cottage garden.

Eventually the mature cottage gardens of the twentieth century would themselves become a source of inspiration to, and an influence on, contemporary garden designers. As with Ireland's country homes and interiors, the cottage gardens, fertile demesnes and flower-filled courtyards also have a part to play in this portrait of Irish country style.

THE PRESENT

Rural Ireland conjures up images of country lanes threading their way through an inspiring blend of mountain, moorland and seascape, scenery of such variety that you wonder how this small island could encompass it all. Bedded down amongst the greenery are thatched and whitewashed farms, stone houses and colourwashed homes: the Irish cottages that gave birth to the country look. Yet, while the charm of the traditional cottage is universal, Irish country people never cared very much for the term. The cottage was a foreign word for their cabin and more closely associated with the picturesque summer pavilions, holiday residences and pretty lodges of the nineteenth-

century English visitor. This was a time when the cottier and his family, often poor, landless labourers scraping an old-fashioned living from an old-fashioned land, lived in debt to the landlord and in fear of the bailiff, and when the cabin or cottage represented more of a curse than a comfort. The reluctant dream was to find the necessary funds to secure a passage to America, Canada or Australia and leave it all behind. Those who emigrated held out little hope of seeing the old place again: it was common practice for them to punch a couple of holes in the sod walls of the empty homestead, fill the building with dry furze and burn it to the ground together with its few sticks of furniture. Harbouring memories like these and associating the cottage with a former life of hardship and poverty, Irish country people traditionally refer to any home as a house.

The appeal of all things Irish, from its homes and houses to its crafts and countryside, attracts many visitors and every year more than three million people choose to cross over to the green isle. There is much to see. In Ireland today there is the occasional crush of spirited supporters come to call up the home side in a Gaelic football match and the odd crowd of optimistic punters planning to risk a punt on an outside chance

RIGHT
Times change. The traditional way of life, pictured here in an isolated Irish cabin near Cloone in County Leitrim, is remembered with affection, but without nostalgia. Instead many elements of past country style, such as the spinning wheel, the inglenook fireplace or the decorative pelmet over the fire, are being revived.

'Mother would cook the meals over the open fire on the crane.
When she had baking to do she'd put it in a pot, stand it on the
crow, a three-legged stand made from three horseshoes, and pile the
coals of burning turf around the pot and over the lid.'

at the famous Curragh racecourse. Yet there is space enough under the wide skies for the solitary angler to dream away his days on a silent Fermanagh lakeside or the solitude-seeking walker to experience the away-from-it-all feel of wandering along an empty country lane with nothing more distracting than the occasional burst of birdsong. As dusk falls there is a good chance of them returning to some quiet house or small country hotel where the beguiling charms of the country style are enhanced by a drop of Irish whiskey and a little story telling around the fire. As Oscar Wilde said of his fellow countrymen: 'We are the greatest talkers since the Greeks.'

Although Ireland has seen more radical social and economic change in the last three decades than it has in the past century, the links between past and present are still strong. Mary Redden, who was born in 1916 on her parent's farm in County Tyrone, well remembers the way things were. 'Mother would cook the meals over the open fire on the crane. When she had baking to do she'd put it in a pot, stand it on the crow, a three-legged stand made from three horseshoes, and pile the coals of burning turf around the pot and over the lid. And if we was ever to get in trouble, she'd threaten to fetch down Sweet Lips as she called it, the willow wand which hung over the brace on the chimney.'

In a place where people have held fast to the traditional pace of life for far longer than in neighbouring Europe, the country style with its hand-crafted furniture and vibrant colour schemes has often been quietly incorporated into the every-day way of things. Country people and their city cousins were content to keep the old Belfast sink, the practical kitchen dresser or the kitchen range. This was partly because, if it had not gone wrong, there was no call to change it, and partly because people had a genuine fondness for fixtures, fittings and furnishings with an ancestral, hand-me-down history.

Away to the west in a quiet hamlet near buoyant Galway city, Patrick and Norah are learning to take life a little easier now that their family have outgrown them. With sons in America and daughters in England, the couple still live in the plain-looking bungalow built by Norah's father with its stone-walled garden and curiously decorated porch. Inside, while the television, stereo set and microwave oven anchor the scene firmly in the late twentieth century, details survive that Mary Redden would instantly recognize from her own youth eighty years ago: the faded brocade of a comfortable armchair beside the fire; a kettle simmering on the cooking crane over an open fire of smouldering peat; a pine table stood by convention beneath the window which overlooks the garden. Outside, near Patrick's new car and the freshly whitewashed pillars of the garden gates, a painted, cast-iron pump stands over a well. 'We have the mains water now, which is fine enough,' explains Patrick, 'but there's no harm in a drop of the well water for drinking.' A living link between the nineteenth and twentieth century, Patrick and Norah's house blends comfortably into the surrounding landscape. The same cannot be said for the unplanned rash of bungalow building which has blighted the view in parts of rural Ireland or for other undesirable legacies of the twentieth century such as urban sprawl or heavy traffic. Nevertheless most of Ireland remains a place of peace and tranquillity and a country which has managed to maintain its green credentials.

Irish gardens, which have gained an international reputation and become places of pilgrimage for gardeners worldwide, meanwhile continue to grow and prosper. The Irish government's Great Gardens' Restoration Scheme, which has uncovered a horticultural treasure trove of old gardens, has added to the stock of 'gardens, where the soul's at ease', as the great Irish poet William Butler Yeats would have it.

THE FUTURE

Country styles throughout the western world are regularly resurrected and rejected by stylists and designers. Some, such as the cool French country or the persuasive Shaker look, have survived the mood swings of fashion, while elsewhere country styles have restlessly disappeared and reappeared as the traditionalist and the avant-garde argue over their respective merits. In the late nineteenth century, for example, the leaders of the Arts and Crafts movement, and men like William Morris, were urging architects and homeowners to learn from the instinctive simplicity of old English country style which the previous generation had dismissed as the mere craft of peasantry. Now such styles have found favour once more: repaired, recycled and reproduction architectural elements, classic crafts, hand-finished furnishings, handmade furniture and traditional decorative techniques such as stencilling, colourwashing and liming have again become a source of inspiration to the contemporary homeowner. The rootstock of these ideas still rests with their country origins, in the traditional way an Ulsterman shaped his hearth, a Munsterman painted his walls, a Connaughtman formed his windows or a Leinsterman his doorway.

It would take a book ten times the size of this one to detail all the distinctive differences between the architectural character of the four Irish provinces of Munster, Ulster, Leinster and Connaught. But it is well within the scope of the sensitive house restorer to research his or her own neighbourhood style and, rather than add another mutilated mistake to the housing stock, restore a home which slips as harmoniously into the landscape as its predecessors did.

The integrity of any building relies on the lie of the roof, the look of the walls and, perhaps most important of all, the design and style of its doors and windows. Irish windows range from the sliding sash of a thatched mansion in County Cavan to the semi-circular Diocletian window of some old Ulster rectory. Replacing any of these with a sea of glass gripped in a white

plastic frame gives a grotesque twist to the term 'restoration'.

Adopting a similarly sensitive approach to interior decorations and furnishings will not only delight the house guests, but also help to prevent the old home being turned into a travesty of its former self. Colour is both the least expensive and the most effective element in decoration and in Ireland it was always used to good effect. In the south-west especially, the custom of washing the outside of a house in exuberant and sometimes startling colours continues to this day. Inside the home too, the use of colour was often bold and unrestrained. When twentieth-century interior designers were advocating a unified approach to colour, with the colour scheme in one room dutifully conforming to those in the rest of the home, the Irish householder continued to use contrasting colours in neighbouring rooms and to paint a bright finish on furniture

LEFT
The Gothic style was originally exported from northern France in the twelfth century, but it enjoyed a revival in nineteenth-century Ireland and led to some distinctive details such as this window. Often charming, and sometimes eccentric, architectural features like these are well worth restoring and preserving.

RIGHT
Lichen-patterned walls in an Irish country garden surround an old hand pump and weatherworn stone trough. Traditional treatments such as these are preferable to adopting each new look that comes along. Architectural salvage or good quality reproductions are preferable to off-the-shelf solutions.

and other interior woodwork. Now modern paints are being used to recreate those effects. The powdery translucence of traditional distemper, for example, can be reproduced with modern water-based emulsions and gouache, while doors, dado rails, panelling and skirting can be coloured with specialist wood paints to recreate the look that was once an integral part of the Irish interior.

Adapting to the traditional character of a house and garden rather than feverishly clothing it in each new look which comes on to the market has distinct advantages: modern doors and windows, fitted cupboards and fashionable furnishings do not always delight the eye, nor age so well as restored or repro-duction pieces; and just as the traditional features of country style suit a period house better than most modern treatments, these same elements can also improve the good looks of a new

home. A contemporary country-style kitchen with a cast-iron stove, comfortable wooden chairs and refrigerator and dishwasher discreetly concealed behind a pair of well-worn deal doors can be just as inspiring as the carefully preserved interior of some eighteenth-century thatched manor with its earth-coloured walls, flagstone floors and wide open fire-place. In order to achieve the look of the Irish country style, homeowners nowadays are sourcing architectural salvage and reproduction materials rather than relying on off-the-peg fixtures and fittings, adopting traditional renovation techniques rather than instant, fix-it solutions; and simply learning to live with low-hanging beams or the gentle undulations of a limewashed wall. In Ireland people have once again come to value their own sometimes charming, sometimes eccentric, but always intriguing Irish country style.

'There's not a house or window,

there's not a field or hill,

But, east or west, in foreign lands,

I'll recollect them still.'

'The Winding Banks of Erne'
WILLIAM ALLINGHAM

Irish Country

Fungus on a fallen tree, above, and,
opposite, a stream coursing down the hillside
towards Connor Pass and Mount Brandon in
County Kerry. The origins of country style
have their roots in rural Ireland, a place
patterned by history and imbued with legend.

WHILE THE THEME OF IRISH COUNTRY STYLE has been seamlessly assimilated into contemporary designs and interiors, its origins lie in the traditions of rural life and the character of the Irish countryside. Shaped and weatherworn during prehistory into the mild, green place it is now, this is the landscape that provided the natural materials and the resonant colours associated with Irish country style. However, it was the people's history, heritage and architecture that gave form to the style.

IRISH LANDSCAPE

A schoolchild's summary of the Irish landscape will have it that this island, its mountains rimming a muggy pool of peat, looks like a saucer floating in the sea. His or her geography teacher might more accurately describe the topography as marked by several low mountain ranges, which broadly surround a central region of marshy lowlands and peat plains. He could add that Ireland is around 480 km (298 miles) long, 270 km (165 miles) wide and that no one lives further than 112 km (70 miles) from the sea. Such a dry summary does not explain why this island should possess more than 150 wildlife sanctuaries, nor account for the enduring appeal of its countryside. Ireland is a place of soaring seaside promontories decorated with pink thrift and white sea campion; of lush lowlands, the hedge banks a profusion of blackberry, gorse and

ragged robin; of heather-covered moors in the margins of the grey, brooding mountains and in the mountains themselves; and of lakes and wetlands teeming with fish and edged with water lobelia and the dancing yellow heads of fleabane.

The hand of man was already shaping this rich land eight thousand years ago, and the land fed the people, continuing to do so until the catastrophic crop failure and the ensuing Great Famine of the 1840s. Nevertheless at the turn of the last century the majority of the population still relied on agriculture for their daily bread – today no more than a quarter do – and a mixture of caution and economic necessity led many to maintain their traditional farming methods long after they had disappeared from the British mainland. Apart from avoiding serious pollution and providing distinct benefits to wildlife – threatened species of wild birds such as the corncrake and chough are still common enough in the west of the country – this adherence to tradition, especially among older Irish people, has conserved a rich country culture far longer than in most of Europe.

CLIMATE AND COLOUR

The Celtic folk who first settled in Ireland more than two and a half thousand years ago had a passion for multicoloured jewellery. The Celtic colours are still there in the dun brown of the bracken hillside, the raw sienna of the bog marsh and the Indian yellow of the loughside rushes, colours that remain an inspiration to the landscape artist and photographer. Yet there is more than a grain of truth behind the flight of fancy which led the eighteenth-century Belfast man, William Drennan, to describe his country as the Emerald Isle. Green is both the notional and the natural colour of a country, which is said to contain forty shades of green at least. There is the green slice of the Irish Republic's tricolour, the blaze of green bunting which erupts on St Patrick's Day, and the olive green of the horse-racing turf.

Nine hundred years ago the great green expanse of the Irish

RIGHT

A temperate climate and abundant rainfall has served to make Ireland a green and pleasant land. Here sheep graze the green sward above the saltwater Strangford Lough in County Down where Feehary Island lies marooned in Ballymorran Bay.

pasturelands prompted the travelling monk Giraldus Cambrensis to remark that Ireland is 'richer in pastures than in crops and in grass than in grain'. Grass thrives with a generous watering and a temperate climate and the mild Irish weather gives it both. Dublin and the east see an average of 750 mm (30 in) of rain a year while western counties like Galway, Mayo, Kerry and Clare can confidently expect twice that quantity. In the great dairy region of the south-west, the green stuff grows for eleven months of the year. When the farmer pulls his cattle in for the winter it is not because his beasts are going hungry, but to keep them from 'poaching' or trampling the sward into a muddy morass.

Snow sometimes settles on the central mountains, but it is a rare sight in the south-west where exotic plants such as tropical tree ferns and the bog violet of southern Europe mostly survive the occasional frost. What keeps them alive is a curious microclimate, the gift of the lukewarm currents of the gulf stream. Set off west from Donegal Bay and the next land mass will be the Canadian seaboard; take a working passage on an Irish trawler heading north-west from the fishing port of Ardglass, County Down, and the little boat will bucket through more than 1,000 km (620 miles) of sea before reaching the shores of Iceland. Yet despite its exposure to the wild, open expanse of the Atlantic, Ireland is shielded from the polar chill of the north by warm, south-westerly winds. They rise with the gulf stream which, after coursing through the Caribbean and the Gulf of Mexico, crosses the Atlantic and wraps itself around the Irish coast, bringing strange flotsam – a coconut husk here, even a disorientated turtle there – in its wake.

When these warm westerlies collide with the cold polar winds, Ireland experiences its soft days when fine drizzle and low cloud rub out the distant horizons. Very occasionally these soft days will take a turn for the worse and dissolve into blustery storms which rake the shores of the west and north.

Just as the Irish greens are a creation of the climate, so its other country colours are elemental. Silvered stone walls splashed with orange and grey lichens in Connaught; mute black gravestones in a trim Leinster churchyard; brown bracken sliding up the back of a Munster hillside; a dangerous red sunset darkening Malin Head in County Donegal. The

RIGHT

A painted window frames the view from a house in Ballina, County Mayo. Set in a limewashed wall, the sliding sash window is curtained with lace.

FAR RIGHT

The primary purpose of paint is to protect and preserve woodwork. However, like so many of Ireland's exuberant colour schemes, this eyecatching shopfront in Schull West, County Cork was designed to advertise the shopkeeper's wares.

BELOW

The elemental Celtic colours were drawn from nature, from the stones, the flowers and the lichens.

ABOVE

The colours of the countryside in a Donegal tweed. Lichens, leather, leaves and tree bark all yielded natural dyes for colouring wool.

'our mad colour schemes. There is not an ounce of good taste about them,' he declared, 'but they all add up to good fun.'

weather, and the seasons' change, charge this natural palette with startling flashes of colour: a dash of crimson from a hedgerow fuchsia slashing across a country lane in County Mayo; a thread of green, sheep-cropped turf caught in the silvered calm of a Fermanagh lake; a rainbow rising in the dwindling drizzle over bare Ben Bulben in County Sligo; wind-driven white ribbons of surf scudding in over the ultramarine of Bantry Bay in County Cork.

Pictures of the Irish countryside dressed in a dull khaki of green turf and nut-brown bracken do not live up to the true spirit of the place. There are the Christian colours: the clan orange of Protestantism, the cobalt blue traditionally associated with Ireland's most famous citizen, St Patrick, and the white and blue of the Holy Virgin in some wayside shrine.

Then there are the stirring colours of streetside murals and, inevitably down the difficult centuries, the crimson stain of conflict. Although Irish fabrics like Donegal tweed still translate the subtle mountain colours of marl and heather into the warp and weft of their cloth, traditional Irish costume was never a dull affair. The black Kinsale cloak, popular in the nineteenth century, often had a rich, red satin lining; women working the fields in summer liked to wear their hand-embroidered muslin bonnets or rush-weave sun hats. During his stay on the Aran Islands at the turn of the century, the playwright J. M. Synge described scenes which had 'as much variety and colour as any picture from the East'. He was surprised to see the women, poor as they were, dressed in their 'red petticoats and jackets of the island wool stained with madder'.

When ferries dock on the east coast of Ireland, visitors are greeted by the sensible greys of Dublin and Belfast, and the first impression of Irish house colour is that it is sober and restrained. However, moving west into the country, they see the greys gradually giving way to traditional whitewashes and white masonry paint; but slipping off the beaten track they find Irish houses suddenly developing a bold and effervescent colour sense. A modern farmhouse, faced in petal pink, chimneys and all, is set with a deep green door and green gutters; a pair of British-postbox-red barn doors close beneath a battleship-grey, slate roof; and, just once in a while, a modest bungalow is transformed into a homage to the leftover paint pot, decorated with a dash of every colour under the sun with a few extras thrown in for good measure. At the journey's end in the south-west, at towns like Kenmare, County Kerry and villages like Kinsale, County Cork, it seems that every house has adopted its own Mediterranean-style livery, mixing chrome yellows, lime greens, blushing pinks and royal purples in a confident celebration of nonconformity. Constantly researching new colours to satisfy the local market, paint companies catering for the Irish taste face a creative challenge. As one paint manufacturer put it with significant understatement: 'The trend is towards variety.'

It was always so. Long before the introduction of oil-based paints, country homes were regularly washed with distemper, their bright reds and yellow ochres slowly weathering into soft pinks and buttermilks before receiving their next fresh coat. When oil paints became widely available there was a short affair with sky blues, buffs, greens and browns and, while the early twentieth century was briefly characterized by dull overcoats of cream and brown, the vivid old colours, like the language and the music, were already enjoying a revival in Ireland's tourist-struck 1970s and 1980s.

There is great enthusiasm for what one Irish commentator

RIGHT

This yellow-washed house with its low roof, stubby chimneys and solid porch, stands on Achill Island, off the west coast of County Mayo. The house, which evolved from the traditional longhouse, is perfectly designed to keep out the elements.

described as 'our mad colour schemes. There is not an ounce of good taste about them,' he declared, 'but they all add up to good fun.' This affection for strident colour effects was never confined to the outdoors. Being one of the cheapest and quickest ways to transform anything from a worn, wooden desk to a whole wall, a new coat of paint was frequently used to freshen up the interior of the Irish home. It was common practice, for example, when a Catholic householder took their turn to host the Stations and the visiting priest arrived to hold communion and hear confession in the home, that the chairs, tables, walls and ceilings were all given a fresh coat of slow-drying paint. To avoid what some perceived as the monotony of matching interiors, colour schemes often varied from room to room and two-tone combinations were regularly used on the panels of doors, settles, cupboards, the sides of dressers and even the spaces between ceiling joists. Flying in the face of the formal conventions of the big house, contrasting colours were regularly used: light cream with light blue, lemon yellow with lead grey, mist grey with eggshell blue, off white with avocado green. From the paintscapes of country interiors to the bright shopfronts of towns like Kenmare, the Irish use of colour has always been a bold celebration of contrasts.

RAW MATERIALS

A shiny brown dresser, its four shelves packed with sparkling plates, pots and butter dishes and its panelled doors picked out in white paint, stands in the downstairs room of a little one-up and one-down house in Galway city. Now a museum, this was the family kitchen of James Joyce's wife and muse, Nora Barnacle. It is a simple scene typical of the early twentieth-century interiors of rural Ireland. Although in the more affluent farmhouses servants were set to scrub clean the bare white wood of a table top, most Irish country furniture, like Nora Barnacle's old dresser, was painted.

Composing their colours a century ago, country people drew

'as much variety and colour as any picture from the East ... red petticoats and jackets of the island wool stained with madder'

their pigments from local materials, from chalk and soured milk, pig and ox blood, and, of course, the roadside plants of this green nation which were a rich resource. In Counties Donegal and Mayo country children filled their bramble baskets with lichens collected from the rocks of the neighbourhood, which were turned into even, natural dyes. Carrageen moss, heather, ragwort, irises, madder and woad were all harvested for their natural pigments. Heathers from the hillside turned fabrics a clear yellow, madder or woodruff produced a pale red, gorse and ragwort gave shades of brown while a deep blue was derived from woad. Green was difficult to reproduce and even thought to be unlucky by the superstitious, but black was in constant demand. Yellow flag irises made a matt black, chips of oak added to the water gave an even, glossy black and urine mixed with indigo produced a blue-black. However, the simplest way to darken wool was by soaking it in a boghole or boiling it in bog water.

Ireland's bogs form some of the finest peatlands in Europe, as unique as a rain forest and rapidly becoming as rare as a stand of Californian redwoods. They are pretty, unspectacular places, dotted with pyramids of drying turf and crisscrossed by lark song and curlew calls. Pricked with insectivorous blue butterwort, bright yellow tormentil, tufts of cotton grass and the dancing heads of bogbean, the brown bogland which once covered a seventh of the land now faces an uncertain future as mechanical exploitation carries it towards extinction.

Secret treasures slumber beneath the peat. Turfcutters regularly used to find forgotten tubs of butter buried in the bog and would sell them, not as archaeological discoveries, but as high-quality grease for the axles of wagons and carts. A cross-

OPPOSITE PAGE

The family in the byre cottage shared their living space with the animals. In this reconstruction, an Irish dresser from western Ireland stands on its replaceable sledge feet beneath a roof of scraws or turfs.

20

In a land that was short of good growing wood, the resourceful countryman learned to salvage semi-petrified timber from the peat bogs. Cabinet makers could turn the best of it into fine furniture such as this marble-topped table made not from some imported hardwood but from Irish bog oak.

Natural materials and simple solutions served generations of Irish families. Wood turners used unseasoned sycamore to make butter bowls and basins for everyday use, but bog oak, with its ebony-like finish, was reserved for the finer pieces.

section through any Irish bog would reveal a deep slice of history. Eight-thousand-year-old hazel, oak and elm lie beneath the remnants of the fields of Stone Age farmers. Above, a deep litter of pine from Ireland's old coniferous forests was overlaid by the swamp vegetation which turned to peat and still holds secrets of the past – a Bronze Age cooking pit, a hoard of Celtic weapons, even a perfectly preserved corpse.

The bogs have been exploited by the resourceful countryman for several thousand years. As well as being used to dye wool, the boglands provided peat for the home fires; sphagnum moss was widely used as a first-aid field dressing during the First World War; semi-fossilized bog timbers were regularly used for building work; and turfs, laid across the house roof, gave the householder a cheap and highly efficient form of roof insulation.

WOOD

Timber salvaged from the bogs sometimes found its way on to the kitchen fire (it still does in County Donegal) although more often it was sold on for a little tobacco money. Larger timbers were taken for joists, rafters, purlins, lintels and door frames. Small branches formed a supportive layer for the bed of scraws or sods that was laid under the thatch of the house roof, while roots and twigs could be soaked and twisted into rope. The most durable and expensive wood was reclaimed from the boglands, the collectors tracing the submerged oak, yew or fir by the absence of dew on the surface of the bog above. Best bog oak, with its distinctive black sheen and a finish like polished ebony, was, and still is, prized by cabinet makers and carvers who would dry the wood, carve it and then finish it with sandpaper and beeswax.

Rescuing semi-petrified timbers from the bogs was a laborious and sometimes dangerous business, but it had to be done because Ireland's indigenous woodlands had been sold for a song long ago. Many Irish place names confirm that this country was once as thickly wooded as the wastes of Scandinavia. Youghal in County Cork was not only the place where Sir Walter Raleigh is supposed to have planted Ireland's first potato; it was also, as its Gaelic name suggests, the 'place of the yew wood'. (Another of Youghal's arboreal tales concerns

the lively Countess of Desmond, said to have perished, at the extraordinary age of 147, in a fall from a cherry tree in the town.) Derry is one of Ireland's commonest place names and translates into a 'wood of oak', but even those oaks that were left standing in the mid-seventeenth century had mostly been felled and sold a century later.

Such 'thoughtless prodigality', as one writer put it, which destroyed most of Ireland's woodland, was blamed on the iron masters who fuelled their furnaces with coppiced wood, the builders who assembled so many cage work or timber-frame houses around Dublin and Cork, and the coopers. So insatiable was the coopers' demand for serviceable barrel staves that one Carlow resident recommended that everyone should, like Diogenes, take up residence in a barrel since 'the choycest timber is imploy'd to that use'. In truth the culprits were not so much the coopers and builders, or the iron makers of Draperstown in County Londonderry or Enniscorthy in County Wexford, who wisely managed their renewable resource with an eye to the future, as the farmers with their swing ploughs and mattocks. In the peaceful period between 1700 and the famine of the 1840s the population grew to double what it is today, and any tree which stood on good or poor-growing ground was put to the axe.

By the eighteenth century Ireland was exporting less timber than it was importing from America, the Baltics and Spain, and the cheap imports further devalued the native woodlands. While the fine cabinet makers waited for ship-loads of best mahogany, walnut and ebony from abroad, the jobbing carpenter awaited the arrival of Norwegian and Russian deal or pine. The country carpenter, though, could afford neither and worked instead with off-cuts from the sawmills, empty flax-seed packing cases and even the irregular harvest of foreshore driftwood and shipwreck timber. Furniture making from flotsam was a craft in itself. Carpenters carefully concealed any sea damage, keeping the scarred surface of the wood on the inside or the underside of the furniture and covering the finished article with thick layers of paint to conceal the jigsaw of different timbers. An old country bed, table, chair or chest that has been stripped of paint will often reveal these ancient sea marks.

STONE

Because of the heavy cost of transporting building materials, most country homes and vernacular buildings were constructed from whatever materials lay close to hand, whether it was timber for the carpenter, clay for the brick and tile maker or stone for the mason. In Ireland the volcanic rocks of the north and the sedimentary stones of the midlands and south of the country gave rise to two of Europe's most famous outcrops of stone: the strange basalt columns of the Giant's Causeway in County Antrim and the bare limestone Burren in County Clare where, much to the annoyance of Oliver Cromwell's surveyors, there was neither enough wood for a hanging, nor enough soil for a burial. While limestone lies across most of the Irish midlands, some of the oldest rocks in the country are those of the rugged Donegal highlands, which sweep round from Malin Head in the north before dipping beneath the limestone bedrock and emerging above Galway Bay.

The great bulkhead of black basalt in the north-east is both one of the geological wonders of the world and one of the youngest rock formations. It was formed forty million years ago when molten lava flowed out over the dinosaur-age clays, chalks and limestones, and then froze into monumental and fantastical shapes as it met the cooling seas. The Giant's Causeway is its most famous manifestation, but equally strange are the lesser-known formations such as the Chimney Tops, which was fired on by cannon from the Spanish Armada when it was mistaken for a castle battlement in the half light of evening.

These Antrim lavas were part of a volcanic fault, which passed up through Scotland and out to Iceland, Greenland and the Arctic. Many of Ireland's other rock formations slip beneath the shallow Irish Sea and re-emerge on the British mainland. The stones of the north-west and north-east occur again in Scotland, the rocks of the Wicklow Mountains reappear in Wales and the gentle hill ranges of south-east Ireland

RIGHT

Molten columns of basaltic lava froze into geometric shapes as they emerged on the Antrim coast. A World Heritage site, the Giant's Causeway became a natural attraction, but for the builder, the basalt provided a distinctive house-building stone.

outcrop in south-west England. Despite these landscape sim-ilarities, the hands of the people created a distinctively dif-ferent countryside.

Before they did so the landscape received its final polish during the last Ice Age, when drifting glaciers ground down and rounded off the hills, breached mountain passes like the picturesque Gap of Dunloe in County Kerry and dumped the drumlins of clay and stone that form the hills of County Armagh and the hump-backed islands scattered across the waters of Clew Bay in County Mayo. As these same glaciers stripped the topsoil from the Burren, their melt waters filled the limpid lakes of the interior, creating the vast swampy pools that would eventually be turned into the bogs of Ireland.

Stone is the great resource of the country builder and from the limestones of the great, flat central plain to the granites of Donegal, Galway, Mayo, Down and Wicklow, Ireland offered

– in the past as it does today – a wide choice of building stone. The black volcanic basalt of the north-east could be cut and polished until it looked like black marble; the polished gran-ites of Wicklow served as dressing stone for some of Dublin's fine buildings, while the granites of the Mourne Mountains were turned into the kerb stones and gutters which still line hundreds of kilometres of road at home and abroad.

The Irish earth yielded not only good building stone, but also the precious raw materials which Irish jewellers could craft into beautiful and intricate pieces. The valuable minerals hidden in the Irish hills included gold, from which was made the col-lection of gold neck plates, pendants and torcs at the National Museum in Dublin that makes Ireland look like some El Dorado of the western world. Much of this gold was mined in the coun-ties of Wicklow and Tyrone, and it is still to be found, although in minute quantities, in the Sperrin Mountains of County

Georgian Ireland presents a fine face on the streets of Dublin. While granite from the Mourne Mountains cobbled the roads, the smooth, ashlar stone of the city's Georgian terraces was imported from England through the port of Bristol.

Despite the attractions of imported stone, Irish builders could find a wide range of local stone, from mellow limestone to rock-hard granite. In the 'marble city' of Kerry local limestones were polished to produce the high black shine of this elegant fireplace.

The hills of Ireland yielded precious metals and minerals including copper and gold. Copper, mined in the neighbouring Wicklow Hills, was used to sheath the rotunda of James Gandon's graceful Four Courts, built in 1802 overlooking Dublin's River Liffey.

Tyrone. Irish copper, mined in the Wicklow Hills, sheathed the domes of Dublin's Custom House and Four Courts. When copper was discovered on the Beara Peninsula in County Kerry, more than a thousand miners, many brought over from the copper mines of Cornwall in south-west England, manned the Allihies mines and made the family fortunes of the Puxley family on whom Daphne du Maurier based her novel, *Hungry Hill*. The pastel-coloured houses of the mining village there still stand beneath the rusting remains of the mining gear.

HISTORY AND HERITAGE

The launch of a range of Celtic-style silverware and pewter by London's prestigious retailers Liberty and Co. at the turn of the twentieth century caused a stir of excitement in design circles. Created by the acclaimed designer Archibald Knox, the flowing lines and interlacing of the pieces echoed the Celtic-inspired work of Dublin's Georgian silversmiths whose simple coffee, chocolate and teapots are now rare collectibles. The Liberty launch also brought that loose and inexact, yet instantly recognizable,

Celtic style to an international audience. But the universal appeal of Celtic style was also due to the extraordinary discovery of buried treasure near Ardagh, County Limerick, fifty years earlier. Here a small boy digging the family potato patch unearthed a metal cup which, when it was rinsed under the hand pump, emerged as a dazzlingly beautiful silver chalice decorated with bronze, glass and gold. The boy had stumbled upon one of the most significant hoards of buried treasure ever found in Ireland and the Ardagh chalice, as the prize piece became known, joined other Celtic treasures – brooches, crosses and reliquaries – at the National Museum in Dublin. This unique collection, which still sparkles with the fires of the Celtic craft, continues to inspire contemporary crafts-people, and the Celtic style has continued to exert a profound influence on every aspect of craft work from precious metals and pottery to stained glass and typefaces.

When they first swept across Europe and settled Ireland 500 years before the birth of Christ, the Celts made a distinctive mark on the land-scape with their little farm-steads ringed with banks

ABOVE

*I**n the eighteenth century Dublin's silversmiths were producing dish rings, helmet-shaped jugs and three-legged sugar bowls that were peculiarly Irish. Their craft inspired revivalist designs such as this sugar bowl by Archibald Knox in 1899. When these and other pieces were launched, they sparked a new enthusiasm for the Celtic style.*

The graceful Ardagh Chalice, found buried in a potato patch in 1868, was made over 1300 years ago. It ranks as one of the finest pieces of Early Christian metalwork.

ABOVE

More than two thousand years old, this golden armband illustrates the cultivated arts of Celtic craftspeople.

ABOVE

Pieces such as this ancient torc of Celtic gold continue to inspire contemporary Irish craftspeople.

LEFT

With its sophisticated closing mechanism, the Broighter gold torc or neck collar, found in a gold hoard in County Londonderry, dates back to around the third century BC. It is part of the collection at the National Museum, Dublin.

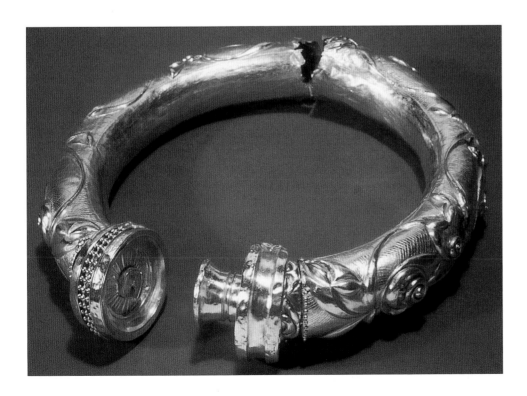

and ditches and their hilltop stone forts. These raths and cashels took their place among earlier Neolithic monuments such as the ancient passage grave at Newgrange, County Meath, its stones carved with inexplicable geometric circles and spirals. Once a year, on the winter solstice, the rising sun falls on a narrow slit above the door lintel and casts a sliver of light on to the floor of the inner chamber. This strange stone clock, more ancient than the Egyptian pyramids, can claim to be the oldest manmade building in the world and shows how skilled architects and astronomers peopled Ireland five thousand years ago. (Country people have a casual and sometimes careless acquaintance with so much prehistory. A friend on a cycling holiday in western Ireland was admiring a standing stone when he fell into conversation with the farmer's red-haired daughter. 'Ah, the stones,' she said, 'they make a terrible nuisance with the tractor. Father has had to dynamite some of the worst to clear the space.')

The Celts, in between battling amongst themselves, took time to impose an early skeletal framework of nationhood across Ireland, establishing their hierarchy of kingdoms under the High King or Ard-Ri. Even when the first evangelizing Christians came to tame their Druidic souls in the third century AD, Celt and Christian settled down together amicably enough. Untroubled by Roman or barbarian attack from the east – neither managed to invade this far west – the Celts and Christians joined forces in an extraordinary flowering of the arts and crafts. With the arrival of the first Vikings, the Celtic nation finally drew to a close in the ninth century. Nevertheless the Celtic influence has remained an essential element of the Irish spirit.

The Normans followed on the heels of the Vikings in 1169 and, having built their solid city walls and castles such as Carrickfergus in County Limerick, brought to Ireland its first system of centralized government. But the seductive qualities of everyday Irish life took their toll on the conquering Normans, who gradually became 'more Irish than the Irish themselves' and by the end of the fifteenth century Norman

'Ah, the stones,' she said, 'they make a terrible nuisance with the tractor. Father has had to dynamite some of the worst to clear the space.'

rule had shrunk to a small region around Dublin.

The English monarch Henry VIII was the first to pronounce himself king of Ireland, in 1541 (although his predecessor Henry II had had his Lordship of Ireland confirmed by the pope over 300 years before). Ever afterwards, Ireland's history would be marked by the struggle of native and settler alike against colonial rule. In a succession of dramatic events which, depending on the political persuasion of the storyteller, made or marred the nation, Ireland experienced a succession of uprisings, rebellions, liberations, suppressions and civil wars which damaged or destroyed much of old Ireland. The Plantation of Ireland, for example, in the sixteenth and seventeenth centuries saw the estates of the native Irish taken away by the English crown and handed over to land-hungry Presbyterian Scots and Anglican English settlers, the planters. It turned the north of the country into a Protestant enclave, introduced new cultures and customs and caused repercussions which have resounded to this day.

One consequence (and a source of mystery to most visitors) was the 1921 Anglo-Irish Treaty, which separated Northern Ireland from what would become the Republic of Ireland. The four Irish provinces, Ulster, Connaught, Leinster and Munster, are made up of thirty-two Irish counties. Under the treaty, the Northern Ireland border was drawn through Ulster, separating three of its counties, Donegal, Cavan and Monaghan, from the Six Counties of Northern Ireland; the six, with Belfast as their regional capital, remained under British rule. The remaining three counties, with the twenty-two of the other three provinces, officially became the Republic of Ireland in 1949, with Dublin as the seat of government.

Despite the religious feuding which has made headlines across the globe, confrontation is not a feature of country life and the people's history, still largely unrecorded, tells a different story of evolving tradition and of a mostly harmonious coexistence between Protestant and Catholic. One of the many stories of quiet co-operation concerns the threat to a Protes-

Peat to fuel the home fires is still gathered today, as it has been for centuries, by hand. The peat, or turf, is cut into bricks and stood in stacks to dry.

tant church in St Mullin's, County Carlow. Alarmed that a visiting bishop might close their friends' church because of its dwindling congregation, local Catholics secretly swelled the ranks of the Protestants at prayer during the bishop's visit, and the church was saved.

It was not only economic necessity that forced millions to leave their country and settle abroad. The one common experience of almost every Irish family was emigration, prompted by religious and political persecution as well. By the mid-nineteenth century a fifth of all Canadians were Irish; today forty-two million Americans, almost a third of all Australians and one sixth of New Zealanders can claim Irish descent. Many of the original emigrants came from the hard-pressed west and south-west, and most took with them mementoes of the old country ways from the favourite country dresser or kitchen settle to hand-me-down songs and tales of how life used to be.

In the final half of the twentieth century, Ireland and its expanding economy gained a reputation as the Emerald Tiger of Europe as it established itself as one of the key countries in the European alliance. Yet the Irish still hold firm to their identity – it would be futile to try to hide a small Cotswold parish among the mountains of Mourne or a Breton clos behind the bare, grey hills of the Burren: the absence of whitewashed porches and stone gateways, of odd lodges and eccentric gatehouses, of cottage halls and polite parlours would soon give the game away.

COUNTRY ARCHITECTURE

Many of Ireland's architectural gems were destroyed during the country's turbulent past. Oliver Cromwell's forces sacked castles, monasteries and whole towns in the mid-seventeenth century and in the bitter years of the early twentieth century many grand houses of the old Anglo-Irish landlords were destroyed. Puxley Castle, a half-chateau, half-Italianate extravagance, built by the Puxley family near Castletownbere echoing the verse of one of Mrs Alexander's hymns:

The rich man in his castle,
The poor man at his gate,
God made them high or lowly
And order'd their estate

was one such casualty, burned to the ground in the 1920s. Some of the Georgian legacy remains, however. The consecutive reigns of kings George I to IV coincided with the artistic and architectural fashion for classicism, from the early

ABOVE

A fanlight like a peacock's tail provided a fitting finish to the Georgian doorway. The restrained uniformity of the Georgian era was not confined to the elegant squares of Dublin, and the real legacy of Georgian Ireland lay in the countryside where so many box houses were built.

OPPOSITE PAGE

The ruins of Tyrone House testify to the country's turbulent past. Economic disasters and sporadic social unrest have regularly robbed the island of both the vernacular and the grander homes. Now, however, many of Ireland's old buildings are undergoing sensitive renovation and restoration.

eighteenth century to the mid-nineteenth century. Dublin, with its elegant Georgian squares and famous fan-lit doorways, is sometimes seen as the period's finest example, but the real backbone of Georgian Ireland rests with the abundance of box-like, minor mansions which were so favoured by the ruling gentry of the time (and which, for the same reason, were so often destroyed in the years to follow).

More recently, it has been lax planning controls and economic imperatives, rather than social protest, that have seen so many of Ireland's large, old houses disappear beneath the developer's concrete. Ireland's folk architecture, meanwhile, has sometimes suffered a similar fate. There are two conflicting images of country architecture in modern Ireland. The creaking stand of postcards revolving in the breeze outside most tourist shops paints a picturesque portrait of rural life: a black, sit-up-and-beg bike leaning against the limewashed walls of a thatched farmstead; whitewashed cabins sparkling under blue skies; a mournful donkey carrying a kelp-filled pannier down a country lane. Although such scenes survive, most country towns are encircled by a necklace of bungalows that, with their fancy verandas and dashing red roof tiles, have more of the hot hacienda to them than the traditional turf cutter's cabin.

As the classic thatched and limewashed country cabin fell out of favour in the last half of the twentieth century, the more comfortable bungalow regularly replaced it.

Like the country harvest, country house building was once a neighbourly business in which friends and family often joined forces to build a new home. Arrangements might be made on the evening of the meitheal, the harvest festival, when the farmer, his corn safely stored and ready for threshing, could tell from a glance at the moonlit ricks whether he could afford to build a new home during the approaching winter. News of a rush of home building became a favourite topic of conversation over a drop of poteen at the annual meitheal in the 1880s when the first public housing initiative in the British Isles saw thousands of one-roomed, roadside hovels demolished and replaced by fifty thousand solid little cottages.

The contemporary appeal of a quiet country life, of cultivating a kitchen garden away from the strains and stresses of the city, is a far cry from the experiences of many turn-of-the-century families. Their traditional homes, with their calcimined walls gleaming like a beacon against the green hills, concealed some dark secrets inside. A census in 1861 revealed that of a population of almost four and a half million, three and a half

However picturesque it might have seemed to outsiders, no one wished to live beneath the tin roof and tumbling thatch of a dilapidated cottage. Like these donkeys with their wickerwork creels, below, this way of life is a thing of the past.

The rudiments of Irish country style, seen here at Ulster's Folk and Transport Museum, have been recreated in folk museums across Ireland. Now, from the turf fire and the pine table to the brass bedstead in the bedroom beyond, features such as these are being brought back into the Irish home.

million lived in single-roomed, mud cabins. They did not live alone. One Sligo civil servant described how a sick farmer, his wife and five children shared a home no larger than a modern garage with their three cows, two calves, two pigs, one horse and the poultry.

Half a century later a new book of house plans, *Bungalow Bliss*, became an even more popular topic of conversation. The single-storey, low-lying bungalow was promptly adopted as the ideal design and seen as being so close in character – if not in appearance – to the traditional, two-roomed cabin that it made an immediate and devastating impact. There was no great nostalgia for the old place, which was often reroofed with corrugated tin and turned into a tool store or animal shed when the new bungalow was built.

Nevertheless the changes inside these modern country homes were less dramatic. The innate conservatism of country people meant that there were no complaints about the per-

formance of the old dresser, the ladderback chairs or the bogpine table. The settle or saddle bed still served a useful function, seating up to eight around the turf stove; and since it opened at night into a bed for the one or two guests who stayed over, it was also often given house room.

In the last half of the twentieth century there was a dawning realization that by allowing too many of the old houses to be destroyed, Ireland risked losing one of its most attractive assets. People began to take a fresh look at Ireland's vernacular architecture and to turn their creative attention to renovating and conserving elements of Irish country style. Many newcomers, seduced by the charm and quality of Irish country life, enthusiastically took on the renovation and restoration of traditional Irish homes. These buildings are a crucial part of Ireland's historical jigsaw, an echo from the past and a lesson in economy for the future. It would be a tragedy to lose them.

'The Irish, by tradition, were free in spirit if
not in reality and these model villages were, if
anything, more like a straitjacket than
some liberating Utopia.'

The Irish Province

*Thatched and whitewashed cottages such as
this traditional cabin in Ballyconneely,
County Galway, present an archetypal image
of old Ireland. But each of Ireland's four
provinces, Connaught, Ulster, Leinster and
Munster, has its own brand of landscape,
character and country architecture. The
barn, above, is in County Sligo.*

ANY COUNTRY STYLE, be it African or American, English or Italian, is an amalgamation of its regional designs and traditions. Just as French country style encompasses elements from Brittany to Provence so does Irish country style rely on the distinctly different contributions of its four provinces, Connaught, Ulster, Leinster and Munster. Travel clockwise through the provinces and the country buildings seem to change as often as the weather: tight thatched cabins in Connaught, sober, slate-roofed houses in Ulster, weatherworn thatched mansions in Leinster and bold, colourwashed cottages in Munster.

Despite a minor epidemic of bungalow building in the past thirty years, the small Irish house still makes a memorable mark on these green landscapes. Ireland's vernacular farms and houses were built with function rather than fashion in mind. They evolved gradually and organically – conservative though country people were, they were always open to new ideas – and it is often possible to trace the origins of an older house in some apparently modern country cottage. Unlike the fine imported mahogany and Portland stone of the grand houses, local materials dictated the look of these unpretentious country homes. Where building stone was lacking, the good earth itself sufficed. In the south and east of Leinster and Munster local clays and mud were used to form walls as solid as those of any cob cottage across the Irish Sea in the English West Country. In the north and west it was the local stone that served

the housebuilder's needs, although the poorer stuff needed a good whitewash to weatherproof it. Thatch was once common across the country and by no means reserved for the humbler homes. It survived far longer in the land-hungry counties of the west than in the soft, rich pastures of the east. Here the farmers were already busy slating their roofs at the turn of the twentieth century – while Ireland is divided by the administrative border separating north from south, there were always deeper social and economic divisions between the east and west of the country. Until relatively recently, the main approaches to Ireland were from the north-east, the east and the south-east. Whether it was a conquering Viking arriving from southern Britain, or an itinerant artist travelling from western France to earn his living with a little local stencilling, the incomer met first with the open, level and fertile lands of Leinster and Munster. And it was here among the small townships and little hamlets that new ideas were seeded and new materials traded. The western regions including most of Ulster, the far west of Munster and Connaught were more rugged and less accessible. They retained the old ways here for far longer and they continued to turn a traditional face on the world for far later than their neighbours to the east.

CONNAUGHT

The remote mid-west of Ireland forms part of the province of Connaught, which embraces Counties Galway, Roscommon, Leitrim, Sligo and Mayo, where a few whitewashed cottages still lie scattered along the Atlantic shoreline, their thatch lashed down against the gables with ropes and boulders.

In County Galway a necklace of lakes, Loughs Conn, Mask and Corrib separates the wilder west of Galway from the deep sheep and cattle pastures and tidy limestone villages of the east. Iarconnaught, one of the bastions of Gaelic, the Irish language, lines the north coast of Galway Bay, caught between the Atlantic Ocean and the shadow of the Maumturk Mountains.

Irish is a Celtic language and the survivor of successive waves of cultural invasions from the east. An Irish speaker might manage to understand a Welsh, Scottish, Breton or even a Basque speaker, for these western parts of Europe are all hardy remnants of the Celtic culture. In Ireland steps were taken to revive the Irish language in the 1920s and now, in these Irish-speaking, or Gaeltacht areas, more than seventy per cent of the population speak Irish.

On the Aran Islands too the Gaelic is as resilient as the web of dry stone walls which grips the mosaic of little fields and where tradition seems determined to resist the march towards the twenty-first century. Galway people have a special talent for dry stone walling, fitting the jigsaw of rocks together in houses where the walls may be as much as a metre wide at the base. This west coast is a place of close-knit communities and dual-purpose homesteads, where the farmer kept a boathouse and the fisherman a barn; and a place where customs, like fireside tales, are remembered from generation to generation. One enduring tale concerns the Claddagh ring, a distinctive silver or gold design of two hands holding a heart. Passed down from mother to daughter, the Claddagh ring was often the one major investment a hard-pressed fishing family could afford. The man who knew its secret could tell at a glance from the way the ring was worn whether or not the wearer was spoken for. The three thousand strong community of Claddagh was swept away by the suburbs of Galway city and now only the story of the ring remains. Although the people of Claddagh are gone, the fisherfolk of Dunbuleaun Bay down the coast from Galway city still harvest the 285 hectares (700 acres) of river and seabed, which are the source of the famous Clarinbridge oysters, and every September Galway people join the tourists to sup shellfish and beer at the oyster festivals.

Criss-crossed by stone walls and hedges bursting with native fuschia, neighbouring County Mayo also has its communities of Irish speakers or Gaeltacht: places like Carrowteige and Toormakeady on the shores of Lough Mask. Mayo, like other parts of Connaught, has a generous share of cashels and old castles, though not all Connaught castles are conventional: the castle in a forest clearing near Monivea, County Galway, is the miniature marbled mausoleum of Robert Percy Ffrench, who built the neighbouring linen weavers' village of Monivea.

As the bright dry stone walls of the west give way to the network of green hedgerows and fertile fields of eastern and southern Connaught, the whitewashed faces of the rough stone cottages give way to houses built of strong limestones and soft

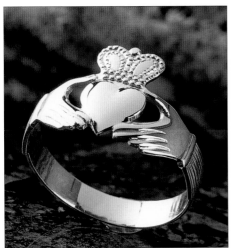

The secret symbolism of the Claddagh ring was not only concealed in its design, but also by the way in which it was worn. More than a mere souvenir, the betrothal ring is a relic of the close-knit, Gaelic-speaking fishing community that was once part of Galway.

The province of Connaught encompasses Counties Galway, Roscommon, Leitrim and Sligo as well as the bright and buoyant streets of Galway City itself. Gaelic is still the first language of almost half the people who live in County Galway.

The stonemasons of Connaught perfected their art on the churches and gravestones. It was a craft brought to perfection in the intricately carved tympanum over the doorway of Clonfert Cathedral.

Thoor Ballylee, restored by Ireland's most famous poet, William Butler Yeats, looks across the woods and farmland of Gort in County Galway.

sandstones. Here the craft of the old stoneworkers immediately becomes more apparent. At Clonfert in County Galway the sandstone was sufficiently supple to be carved into the grotesque Romanesque heads and faces to be found over the doorway of Clonfert Abbey, while to the east the limestone was easily split and shaped into basic building blocks for the solid little whitewashed houses.

The rural tranquillity of modern Mayo's pasture lands masks the historical hardships of the mid-nineteenth century, when, as in other parts of the western Ireland, high rents and evictions came close on the heels of the famine. Long after the tragedy many Connaught people were forced to abandon their homes and pastures to seek a new life overseas, and heritage centres here and across Ireland have been set up to help people trace their Irish roots. One name, which needed no research, was that of Captain Charles Boycott, the infamous land agent who stubbornly resisted a campaign by the National Land League to reduce tenants' rents to more manageable levels. The men of Mayo in their turn refused to bring in his harvest and the term boycott was born.

One of Connaught's more tolerant sons was the poet William Butler Yeats. He, like his brother, the painter Jack Yeats, spent his childhood holidays among the enticing scenery of County Sligo where he nurtured a lyrical awareness of the native beauty of home-grown architecture and he wrote in his poem, 'The Lake Isle of Innisfree':

> *I will arise and go now, and go to Innisfree,*
> *And a small cabin build there, of clay and*
> *wattles made.*

The clay and wattle cabin never was built at Innisfree, the little island on Lough Gill in County Sligo, although Yeats did restore a ruined sixteenth-century tower house,

> *With old millboards and sea-green slates*
> *And smithy work from the Gort forge*

at Thoor Baylee near Lough Coole, County Galway. And when his dead body was brought back from France and laid to rest under sheer, bare Ben Bulben's head, the massive limestone outcrop that towers over his final resting place, his epitaph was inscribed as he instructed, not on dressy marble or polished slate, but on a piece of local limestone quarried near the spot.

> *Cast a cold eye*
> *On Life, on death,*
> *Horseman, pass by!*

Connaught's literary associations are as nothing compared to its religious ones. Every year pilgrims converge on Knock in County Mayo to worship at the site of the late-nineteenth-century vision of the Virgin Mary. Away to the west others toil up Croagh Patrick, some of them barefoot, to the sacred summit where St Patrick once sounded his holy bell and drove the snakes and toads – all but the natterjack toad – to leap to their deaths and abandon Ireland for ever.

Croagh Patrick and Ben Bulben gaze down on the old homes of Connaught, the low-lying, whitewashed cabins of the west and, looking like grown-up versions of the cottages, large farms extended in length and height rather than breadth. Many farms and smallholdings have two yards, the one at the back surrounded by low outbuildings and reserved for the daily work of the farm, the yard at the front filled with shrubs and flower-

A boxed-in wall bed, built into an alcove beside the hearth, is a feature common to many of Connaught's old farmhouses.

beds. Cottage and farmhouse alike sometimes retain the characteristic kitchen alcove with its bed built into the back wall and curtained off from the hearth.

Although common sense dictated native designs like these, few householders were immune to new and fashionable ideas. Whether they were invited to the 'big house' for some celebration or simply brought there to wash the master's linen, the homesteader and his wife were exposed to a life of affluence and high fashion: elegant drawing rooms decorated with Grecian friezes and handsome Chinoiserie wallpapers; graceful hallways hung with chandeliers and lined with Georgian mouldings; ornate gateways and towering chimneys. Gradually architectural elements from the grand houses began to filter down the social scale. In the late eighteenth and early nineteenth centuries the farmer might add an extra chimney, which served no fire below, to an old farmhouse just for appearance's sake. His wife, meanwhile, collected the items she needed to furnish her smart new parlour, often simply referred to as 'the room'.

In Connaught there were even social parallels in the Irish version of the sauna. While the well heeled might relieve their aches and pains at Kilcullen's Bath House in Inishcrone, County Sligo, relaxing in the 2 m (7 ft) long porcelain tubs filled with seaweed and hot water, the country alternative was to use a roadside hot house. Some eighty small stone buildings, where people would sweat out their rheumatism and sciatica on the hot clay floor before hobbling into a nearby stream to cool down, survive beside the country roads which weave round County Leitrim's loughs and rivers.

ULSTER

Although in 1921 the Anglo-Irish Treaty divided the province of Ulster, placing Antrim, Down, Armagh, Tyrone, Fermanagh and Londonderry, the Six Counties, in Northern Ireland and leaving counties Donegal, Cavan and Monaghan over the border in the Republic, the historic province encompasses the nine counties. The Six Counties may still be part of the British kingdom, but paradoxically they carry more Gaelic place names than any other area. The powerful chieftains who ruled Ulster right up until the seventeenth century fiercely preserved the region's Gaelic identity. The planters who took over the lands

RIGHT

The province of Ulster stretches across the north from County Donegal in the west to busy Belfast in the east. Here at Gortahork, east of County Donegal's Bloody Foreland, thatched and whitewashed farmhouses overlook the sandy strand. Crofters like these often supplemented their income with weaving.

held on to, and anglicized, the names so that today there are still common Gaelic references in the north such as Ard (a height), Bally (from *baile*, a townland) and Drom or Drum (a ridge).

Unspoiled Donegal, for most visitors the least familiar of the Irish counties, lies to the west where the north Atlantic breakers roll in against its craggy coastline, drenching colonies of cheerful puffins patrolling for fish off Ireland's most northerly point, Malin Head. These same seas pound the feet of the steepest cliffs in Europe, Slieve League, source of the rock-growing fungus crotol which children used to collect to sell to the wool dyers and weavers of Ardara, a centre for handmade tweeds to this day.

Belfast, the focus of Ireland's nineteenth-century Industrial Revolution, lies away to the east, far beyond Donegal's mist-hung Blue Stack Mountains. With its grand opera house, its glittering Victorian pubs and its two giant shipbuilding cranes, Samson and Goliath, which look set to march across the city, big, busy Belfast seems far removed from the serene charms of the rural west. Yet, like Donegal, even this city owes its past to the industrious country cottage weavers. Armagh, Dungannon and Belfast formed the linen triangle of the Six Counties, which made more than two million parachutes during the Second World War and which, a century before, was producing half of all the linen in Ulster. When in the seventeenth century Protestant Huguenots fled France, many boarded the boats to Ireland and finally settled in the soft, south Antrim countryside (joining Scottish and English Plantation settlers, already busy reshaping their seized lands into fertile farm holdings and new towns). This Plantation landscape, however, differs from that of southern Ireland where communities were focused on 'the big house'. Instead the rolling farmland is punctuated by the planned townships of the seventeenth century, each one built and managed by an English merchant company given the task of overseeing the resettlement. When it was granted to a consortium of City of London livery companies, for example, Derry's name was changed to Londonderry. Meanwhile the Drapers' Company was building its own linen towns such as Draperstown and Moneymore with their wide roads radiating out from the diamond-shaped town centres into the neat green

fields and hedgerows of the surrounding countryside.

Lough Neagh, the largest lough in the British Isles, shares its shores with five of the Six Counties of Northern Ireland; County Fermanagh, with its own network of rivers, lakes and loughs interspersed with neat villages and cream and brown, half-timbered houses, lies away to the west. Huge Lough Neagh sparkles with light when seen through the window of an aircraft approaching Belfast (although, because of the low-lying land that surrounds it, it is almost invisible from the ground). North of Lough Neagh lie the plunging Glens of Antrim and, in central Antrim, some of Ireland's richest pastures stretch out beyond Slemish Mountain, the extinct volcano whose grey basalt rock makes its distinctive mark on the blackstone villages of Antrim and County Down. South of Lough Neagh in Armagh, where the soft pink, yellow and red limestone colours the homesteads, nineteenth-century settlers, many of them weavers, founded purpose-built villages like Bessbrook, constructed in 1845 as a model Quaker community with neither pub, pawnshop nor police station. The weavers settled into their solid, slate-roofed houses grouped around the village green while the owner settled his own family in one of Ireland's nineteenth-century, cottage orné-style thatched follies, Derrymore House, which aimed to create a romantic country style without any of its inconveniences. The new towns and villages did not necessarily improve the lot of the locals. As Richard Reid put it in the *Shell Book of Cottages*, 'the Irish, by tradition, were free in spirit if not in reality and these model villages were, if anything, more like a straitjacket than some liberating Utopia.'

In County Down, other grand planters' houses with imposing gateways and beech-lined avenues lie hidden among the winding back roads that link the county's blackstone villages. Mock Tudor Sion Mills in County Tyrone, another nineteenth-

OPPOSITE PAGE

A fisherman's boat lies moored beside one of the finest eel-fishing sites in the province of Ulster. The marshy shoreline of the 400 sq. km (153 sq. miles) Lough Neagh is touched by five of Northern Ireland's Six Counties, a region at the centre of the Irish linen trade.

century planned village for linen workers, was built with its black-and-white, half-timbered workers' houses set in streets shaded with chestnut and beech trees. The half-timbered house was something of a rarity: timber-framed houses, common enough in the seventeenth century, had almost disappeared by the nineteenth century because of the lack of locally available timber.

Not all villages where the linen trade thrived were built for the linen trade: Lislas in County Tyrone had had to be rebuilt when James II, in a fit of pique after his failure to capture Londonderry, had it burned to the ground in 1689. Newtownstewart, which would become another important trading centre for the flax and woollen industries, eventually rose from its ashes in the eighteenth century.

Elsewhere the country homes of Ulster provide yet more reminders of the region's textile past. Before the industrialization of the linen trade, there was money to be made from making linen. The small farmer who bought himself a loom could significantly increase his income and many added a third room for the weaving loom to the back or the side of the typ-

ical two-roomed farmhouse. The banks of the gentle River Lagan, once edged with bleaching greens, the meadows where the naturally grey-brown linen was pegged out to bleach in the sun, are still lined with homes converted from old beetling mills. The mills used to harness the river's flow to power lines of square beechwood beams, the 'beetles', which pounded flat the rounded flax fibres in the woven linen.

Every draper's shop in Ulster kept a stock of good Irish linen. The industrious young draper Timothy Eaton, who later emigrated to Canada, where he established his chain of famous department stores, worked a sixteen-hour day and slept beneath the shop counter in one such draper's shop at Portglenone in County Antrim. The last sight of home for emigrants like Timothy Eaton was the Mourne Mountains, 207 sq. km (80 sq. miles) of solid granite which sweep down to Carlingford Lough in County Down and where the patchwork of farms, with their ladder fields stretching out behind, lies gathered in the folds of land at the mountain's feet. Another Ulster family who left to seek their fortune in the New World was that of James Wilson, grandfather of the American pres-

OPPOSITE PAGE

For many of the emigrants leaving to seek a new life in America, the Mountains of Mourne were the last sight of the famine-torn land. The 'ladder' fields which stretch up to the foot of the mountains near Attica in County Down were a consequence of land reform.

RIGHT

Photographed at the turn of the twentieth century, a family stands by their turf-built cabin in County Londonderry, the thatch roped down against the winds with cords of twisted hay. Such conditions drove thousands from their homeland and gave at least a dozen American presidents a claim to Irish ancestry.

ident Woodrow Wilson. The Wilson family home, thatched with flax over a warm, under thatch of turfs, still stands on the slopes of the Sperrin Mountains at Dergalt, County Tyrone. Inside, the open hearth, kitchen dresser and copper pans paint a telling picture of Ulster country style as it once was. For many of these emigrants and their families, life in an Irish country cottage had been a crowded and claustrophobic experience. The most rudimentary home in the north-east, typically, was the two-roomed cottage built with a front and back door facing one another, designed perhaps so that the draught between the doors would feed the open fire that burned in the centre of the house. Later, when a proper chimney and flue was built to serve the fire, the back door would be blocked up or turned into a window. Elsewhere in the north-east, and in Ulster and neighbouring north-west of Connaught especially, the local cabins followed the style of the vernacular cottages of Scotland from where many of the Ulster settlers originated. These were built with two hearths, one in each gable end, so that both the kitchen and the bedroom opposite could benefit from the warmth of a peat fire.

Woodrow Wilson was one of a dozen American presidents who had Ulster ancestry and other Americans with Ulster roots, listed at the Ulster-American Folk Park near Omagh, are said to include Davy Crockett and Mark Twain; even the first man on the moon, Neil Armstrong, had his roots in Ulster. But one of the most poignant records is that of the Ulster woman Catherine O'Hare who, with the help of Indian midwives, gave birth to the first white child to be born west of the American Rocky Mountains in 1862.

LEINSTER

The Leinster province reaches from the green pastures and brown bogs of the Irish midlands down to the glittering sandy beaches of the south-east. The granite spine of the Leinster hills, which separates the region east from west, runs up from the south, through the Blackstairs Mountains and into the Wicklow Mountains, Dublin's backcloth and, for the novelist H. G. Wells at least, 'the most beautiful view in the world'.

Dublin, city and county, is encircled by the Leinster counties of Louth, Meath, Longford, Westmeath, Offaly, Kildare,

Wicklow, Laois, Carlow, Kilkenny and Wexford, the latter once regarded by Dublin society as beyond the pale both figuratively and literally. The Pale, the military border that surrounded Dublin in Tudor times and now a crossing place for people seeking a quiet life in the peace of the gentle Leinster countryside, is still marked by the fortified manor houses of those troubled times. Driving out of Dublin it is easy to miss Leinster's gentle attractions: its woodland glens, canal-side hamlets and traditional buildings like the fortified tower houses, four or five storeys high, mostly built by prosperous farmers in the fifteenth century and now occasionally given a new lease of life by families looking for an unusual renovation project. At least three hundred have survived in the south-

LEFT

The province of Leinster, which rolls down through the green fields and hills of eastern Ireland, is studded with fortified houses. Dunsany Castle, originally built to defend the Anglo-Norman holdings that bordered the city of Dublin, is a survivor from the twelfth century.

ern counties of Kilkenny, Carlow and Wexford, although most of the ruined castles and ancient monasteries in this deep, green countryside have been beyond repair since they were taken apart by Oliver Cromwell. 'I think we put to the sword two thousand men,' wrote Cromwell after sacking Drogheda in County Louth. 'It is right that God alone should have all the glory.'

Stone and timbers might have been robbed from the broken castles and built into the fabric of nearby homes, but in much of the south, the small country houses were built of clay, mounded up to form solid walls and plastered to keep out the rain. There are two basic building methods for the old vernacular houses: frame construction, where the house is formed from a framework of solid timbers that is then filled with lathe and plaster or brick; and mass construction, where solid walls are built of stone or, as here in the south, of clay. Few frame-built houses have survived in Ireland, although, in Leinster and Munster especially, there is still a good stock of these tempered clay homes, hiding under their protective coats of plaster.

In the basic layout of these two-roomed homes of eastern and south-eastern Ireland, a central wall, opposite the front door, divided the house in two. The fireplace and its chimney were built into this dividing wall and a short projecting wall was built around the fire, invariably with a little spy-hole window let in to it. This convenient arrangement allowed the housewife to leave the front door ajar, tend her fire without a draught on her back, and keep an eye out for callers through the spy-hole window. Curiously many of Ireland's early block- and brick-work bungalows adopted this same ancient design.

Brick was an expensive material for most cottagers until village potters began to manufacture their own in the nineteenth century. On a house where the central chimney was added later in its life, brick would be used for the dividing wall and chimney. Elsewhere a lathe and plaster wall might be used to partition off the rooms of these little homes. Brick was often used to frame the windows and doors of a clay-walled house, although, since glass was a relative luxury in parts of Ireland until late in the nineteenth century, unglazed cottage windows were small, high up in the wall and faced away from the prevailing winds.

The classic country farmhouses of the south-east, long, low and thatched, have a steep hipped roof in contrast to the gabled roofs of the west, the thatch rolling down the end walls. The thatcher relied on what could be harvested from the local countryside for his materials: reed, flax and straw were, and still are, considered a good roof covering, warm in winter and cool in summer. Oat straw was preferred in Counties Louth, West-

meath, Offaly, Kildare and Laois, but heather and even potato stalks have been pressed into service when nothing better was available. The thatch was laid down over an insulating layer of sods on the roof timbers, but the thatchers' methods differed from region to region. The scollop thatcher (scollops were the willow staples used to secure the thatch) of county Louth would finish his roof in a distinctly different way to the traditional thrust thatchers of north Leinster, who wove bundles of knotted straw together to make the roof.

Once the Leinster counties boasted at least one thatcher in every parish, but by the mid-twentieth century Ireland's thatchers were facing an uncertain future as homeowners replaced their thatch with slate, tiles and sheets of corrugated iron. Now the thatchers' fortunes may be returning: although a flax or reed thatch will last perhaps twenty years, with the comb, or ridge, needing attention every five years, some home restorers are reinstating their old thatch roofs, bringing back this graceful-looking roof to the Leinster countryside.

Thatch was far from the minds of the great architects of the eighteenth century, who dressed the Leinster landscape with fine houses such as Castletown in County Kildare,

RIGHT
Thatched farmhouses line a roadside in County Meath. Thatching varied from region to region, and every parish had its own thatcher who would return to patch a roof every five years and renew it every fifteen to twenty years.

The mosaic steps leading to the Italianate gardens at Powerscourt, County Wicklow, were made with pebbles from the beach at Bray. The Palladian mansion, pictured here before its recent restoration, was built in the 1730s, a testament to a very affluent country style.

Russborough House in County Wicklow, built for a brewer's heir in 1741, was designed by Richard Castle. A German architect who settled in Ireland with his Irish-born wife, he was credited with introducing the Palladian style to the Irish gentry.

*A finely decorated niche frames a figure
from Classical mythology in the Long Gallery
at Castletown House, County Kildare.
Built in the early eighteenth century for
William Conolly, Speaker of the Irish
Parliament and then the richest man in
Ireland, Castletown was the work of Italian
architect Alessandro Galilei.*

*The Francini brothers, Italian plasterwork
craftsmen, executed the Rococo-style swirling
scrolls and graceful ornamentation on the
walls and ceilings of the Staircase Hall at
Castletown House. While few could afford to
emulate such lavish styles, many a Leinster
gentleman was persuaded to adopt the
Classical look for his own home.*

Powerscourt near Dublin and Russborough House in County Wicklow. Each was designed to exemplify the chief attributes of Classical architecture: order, proportion, restraint, purity and elegance. It was also the eighteenth century that saw the construction of the network of canals that threaded their way through the countryside and added many tranquil kilometres of waterways to Ireland's 14,500 kilometres (9000 miles) of riverways. The canals of Leinster still offer a serene solution to exploring the province. The Grand and Royal Canals link Dublin with not only the River Shannon and the west coast, but also the beautiful Barrow Line, the navigable river that winds down south to the brightly painted shops and houses of New Ross in County Wexford.

The Royal Canal rises on the Shannon in County Longford and runs through Counties Westmeath and Meath, past Innfield (also known as Enfield after the Great Western Railway Company misspelt its station name), and into County Kildare, home of the Irish thoroughbred race horse and the classic country home, Castletown House. This solid greystone mansion, with one wing reserved for the kitchens and the other for the stables, was modelled on a sixteenth-century Italian palace and became a source of inspiration and envy to other eighteenth-century housebuilders. Local people, more familiar with the old custom of keeping the hens and cattle in one end of the house and sleeping in the other themselves, found employment building the grand house and its lofty folly, which was designed to create work for those struggling through the bitter winter of 1739.

The Royal finally enters Dublin from the north, above the Grand Canal, which leaves the south of the city and passes through County Kildare. Here the Barrow Line branches off and slips south through the luxuriant greenery of Offaly, one of the first counties to be settled by English planters and where the town centre of the county capital Tullamore had to be rebuilt in 1785 after a hot-air balloon exploded, destroying a hundred houses. West of the Barrow Line are the sandstone Slieve Bloom Mountains, which gaze out across pastoral County Laois, described as the Land of the Cow or Achadh Bhó by one monastic settlement and where the red sandstone gives the farmsteads, barns and houses their distinctive good

LEFT

S purning the convention of pebbledash for his bungalow, this householder collected sacks full of seaside shells and used them to decorate the walls and bay window of his cottage in County Kildare.

BELOW

L einster's legacy of grand houses led to the construction of hundreds of gatehouses and lodges such as this one in County Wicklow. Often built as a romantic version of a country cottage, they provided accommodation for servants who were expected to open and close the gates for their employer.

looks. East of the Barrow Line are the valley villages of County Wicklow. At Shillelagh terraces of traditional cottages with decorative door frames and elaborately worked stone porches line the main street of the village. The surrounding oak forests provided the roof timbers for Dublin's cathedral and London's Palace of Westminster, while the village itself lent its name to the fearsome Irish cudgel.

In neighbouring County Carlow the resourceful country-men used the local granite for their Carlow fences, cutting a V-shaped groove in the top of the stone posts to hold the granite slab laid across them. The mushroom-shaped granite stones, often used to decorate Carlow country gardens such as Carrigglass Manor, *below*, once served as staddle stones, which kept rats away from crops stored in the ricks that stood on a circle of the stones. (The durability of the local granite could cause problems: when the doctor who tried to turn Carlow Castle into a lunatic asylum in the nineteenth century used

dynamite to enlarge the windows, he blew the castle apart.)

In the Georgian streets of Kilkenny the eighteenth-century fascination for fanlights over front doors led to the appearance of a single, large fanlight serving a pair of adjoining front doors below. The style seems to have been unique to the 'marble city' of Kerry, so called from the local limestone, which develops a deep, black shine when polished.

The Barrow Line slips on down beside County Kilkenny, past the little Georgian town of Freshford, the pastel-coloured cottages of Inistioge and beyond Thomastown, birthplace of George Berkeley, who gave his name to California's Berkeley University. The River Barrow reaches the sea at County Wexford, a county dotted with pretty villages like Blackwater on the east coast, its cottage walls decorated with sea pebbles, Ballyhack with its colourwashed harbour cottages and Kilmore Quay, a seaside hamlet of thatched and whitewashed cottages.

MUNSTER

Irish people take a great personal pride in the look of their homes. Framing a little sash window with an off-cut of Kenmare lace, finishing the ridge of a thatched roof with an ornamental cockerel made of straw, or decorating the front doorstep with an old skillet pot filled with geraniums are all a matter of design, not accident. The country homes of Munster are a testimony to this attention to detail, especially when it comes to colour.

Rural homes from Mantua to Massachusetts traditionally presented a painted face to the world and with good reason. Sharp colours reflect light and the luminescence of a brightly painted wall helped the householder and visitor to find their way in the starlit dark of a moonless night. But the people of Ireland remained true to their colours long after the arrival of gas and electric light, and nowhere more so than in the province of Munster.

The market towns and little villages of Counties Waterford, Clare, Tipperary, Limerick, Kerry and Cork make up the province. It stretches from the painted, Victorian townhouses of Cobh in County Wexford to the dramatic hills of Kerry; and from the lowland Golden Vale of Limerick and Tipperary to the limestone pavements of the Burren, where cattle graze on the high ground in winter – sensibly enough, since the hills hold their heat and remain warmer than the valley pastures below. Throughout the province bright colours create tonal combinations of startling boldness: a sea-green bench against a pale pink wall; shell-white window frames set in a purple gable wall; a blue-and-white door behind flame-red garden gates. At Cashel in County Tipperary the gaily painted shopfronts and pubs have resolutely resisted the conventional dullness of post-war high-street architecture, while the little Bothàn Scóir, a reconstructed humble home of the seventeenth

ABOVE

A window box of geraniums and petunias vies for attention against the brilliant blue distempered finish of a cottage wall at Kinsale, County Cork. Solutions such as these helped to brighten the home on even the dullest of days.

LEFT

The Mediterranean-like atmosphere of seaside villages in the south-west of Ireland owes more to the house colours than the climate. But places such as Eyeries on the Beara Peninsula in County Kerry benefit from the warming waters of the gulf stream as it winds around the western coast.

century, gives a taste of how life used to be. Like the County Kerry villages of Sneem and Kenmare, the houses of Cashel are in striking contrast to the elegant Georgian doorways and bow windows of Cork itself or the pale limestone which frames the eighteenth-century houses of the old spa town of Mallow, County Cork, once known as the Bath of Ireland.

Apart from its fondness for colour, this corner of Ireland is also home to some curious country buildings. There is a grand, stranded Gothic gatehouse in County Waterford, which was to have led to Ballysaggartmore Towers, had not the eccentric Arthur Kiely, who planned the Towers to rival his brother's mansion Strancally Castle, run out of money on completion

ABOVE

The Burren, from the Gaelic 'rocky land', is the exposed part of a great bed of limestone that ran through the province of Munster and provided good building stone.

of the grey stone lodge and its gateway. The Gothic revival mansion of Strancally Castle overlooks the River Blackwater, upriver from the remains of its predecessor, whose medieval owner is reputed to have acquired neighbouring lands by inviting their respective owners over, cutting their throats and dropping their bodies into the river. North of Strancally near Caher in neighbouring County Tipperary is the cottage orné-style

Swiss Cottage with its fairytale thatch, nineteenth-century Parisian wallpaper and rustic verandas, said to have been designed by the Regency architect John Nash. Dromana Gate, a bizarre mixture of Hindu Gothic, is a more dramatic tribute to Nash and his Taj Mahal-inspired Royal Pavilion at Brighton, England. Built as a temporary structure to surprise the owners when they returned from their honeymoon, it was rebuilt in more permanent materials by the delighted couple and, now rescued and restored by the Irish Georgian Society, has continued to surprise visitors ever since. But Dromana Gate, Swiss Cottage and the unfortunate Mr Kiely's gatehouse are no more eccentric than the odd Cork country bungalow handpainted with a fairground's palette of colour, nor the curious Munster custom of building a gateway at the entrance to any country home, however humble. No smallholding in the west is quite complete without its pair of whitewashed pillars capped with a pyramid or cone and closed by a wrought-iron gate, all once made to homegrown designs.

Regional design is one of the most delightful features of rural life in Munster. While in other parts of Ireland, the conventional two-roomed cottage might be divided by a solid par- tition or wall, here in the west of the region (and up along the western coast) a large dresser or cupboard would serve to separate the house instead. Homemade gates and gaiters, stiles and sickles, wash tubs, well shelters and wheelbarrows were once all made to homegrown designs. In one country community, for example, the traditional half or stable kitchen door is almost unheard of; in another it reigns supreme, while at Tralee in County Kerry, no two doors are alike among the eighteenth-century houses that replaced those destroyed by Cromwell over three hundred years ago.

In Kerry, country people expected to enjoy the heat radiating out from a narrow fireplace as they sat on long wooden forms or benches in the kitchen. In Galway, by contrast, the fireside traditionally took a couple of stone seats set on either side of the hearth to form a cosy inglenook. In the midlands and eastern Ireland the hearth and its solid, squat chimney ran down the middle of the house, dividing the cottage in two; here in the south and west the house usually evolved with a single fireplace on the gable end to warm the long byre cottage which the families shared with their beasts. As these homes were extended, they developed into the long, low farm-

LEFT AND ABOVE

Drawn from nature, the rustic charms of the cottage orné-style Swiss Cottage at Cahir, County Tipperary, are attributed to the Regency architect John Nash.

The last port of call for the first, fateful journey of the Titanic was at Cobh in County Cork. The painted terraced houses were built for the harbour and customs men when Cobh, formerly Queenstown, expanded to cope with the nineteenth-century emigrant traffic to America.

A whitewashed cottage shelters beneath the blue flanks of Brandon Mountain towering over the Dingle Peninsula in County Kerry. Legend claims that St Brendan the Navigator set sail for America after seeing a vision of the 'Land of the Blessed' from Brandon's summit.

houses that are still to be found in the more remote parts of County Clare, with the combined kitchen and living room and its fireplace in the middle of the house and bedrooms at either end. Higher up the social scale, the farmer or gentleman farmer expected a little more of his home in terms of space: 'In 1749 I built a pretty little thatched house ... a parlour, kitchen, cellar, dairy and little hall, three lodging rooms over and garrets,' reported one gentleman from County Cork.

A century later there was little ready money around for such an undertaking. As in western Ireland, this, the south-west, suffered severely from emigration during and after the famine. The final glimpse of home for many was the panorama of Cork harbour and the colourful houses of Cobh. Despite conditions on board boats so crowded they were called the coffin ships, many survived the twelve-week Atlantic crossing, including the impoverished parents of the motor magnate Henry Ford, who left their famine-struck village of Ballinascarty in 1847. Other emigrants were less fortunate: most of those who boarded the *Titanic* as she made her final port of call at Cobh, and who

sailed steerage class on the steamship they believed was unsinkable, perished at sea. It is ironical that the first Irishman to cross the Atlantic – perhaps the first European to reach America – should have done so in a simple, but seaworthy Derry currach well over a thousand years earlier. This was St Brendan, the patron saint of Kerry, whose journey was said to have been inspired by his vision of the Island of the Blessed when he looked west from Brandon Mountain on the Dingle peninsula.

Now, in the closing decades of the twentieth century, colourful Cobh has watched over a reversal in the fortunes of south-west of Ireland as the Cork ferry brings in newcomers from other parts of Europe, arriving to set up home in rural Ireland. The newcomers may have pushed up the price of property and even ruffled a few feathers locally, but many have settled down to pursue their own country livings and have contributed to an upturn in the economy. Since this has triggered a renewed interest in the restoration and preservation of Ireland's homes and gardens, and in the elements of Irish country life, it is a hopeful sign for the future.

'The neighbours at their shady doors swept clean,

Gossip, and with cool eve fresh scents of wheat,

Grasses and leaves, come from the meadows green.'

'A roadside inn this summer Saturday'

THOMAS CAULFIELD IRWIN

Irish Country Life

OPPOSITE PAGE

Ireland's economy is still heavily dependent on its agriculture. While traditional farming scenes such as these, opposite, are gradually giving way to more modern methods, little has changed in the Victorian Crown Liquor Saloon in Belfast, above.

FIFTEEN HUNDRED YEARS AGO, so the story goes, St Columba made an illicit copy of St Finian's psalter. St Finian's demand for its return was backed by the judgement of the High King Diarmud, in what must rank as the world's first copyright ruling: 'To every cow its calf, and to every book its copy,' declared the king. Columba refused to return the book and joined the subsequent Battle of the Books at Coldrumman in AD 561, a war that claimed the lives of more than two thousand monks. Columba won, but, wracked with guilt, fled abroad to repent his plagiarism.

Rural Ireland, with its dramatic scenery, colourful shopfronts, quiet bars and leisured, measured way of life, is unique, and the millions who visit Ireland every year come to sample that uniqueness. They are drawn by strange stories, such as the one about Columba, and by the enduring charms of Irish country life, for Ireland is still predominantly a pastoral country. Only around three and a half million people live in the 6 ½ million hectares (17 million acres) of the Republic of Ireland and the majority of the population, north and south of the border, live in the east, most of them in either Dublin or Belfast.

In Ireland far fewer towns interrupt the rolling green panorama of the countryside than they do in neighbouring England. Parts of the Irish landscape – be it the soaring white sides of Mount Errigal in County Donegal or the island-freckled waters of Lough Corrib, County Galway – are as spectacular as anything the rest of Europe has to offer.

RIGHT
The picturesque prettiness of Adare in County Limerick has relatively recent origins. In the early nineteenth century the poverty-stricken village's neglected cabins were pulled down and replaced with the limewashed walls and rolling thatch of English-style cottages.

But much of it is a working countryside and a trifle dull or unspectacular to anyone other than the farmer (easily identified by his tendency to drive slowly along the crown of the road, inspecting his neighbours' crops and stocks on either side).

While wealthy landowners have tried to mould this land to suit themselves, it was the country people – the farmers, the artisans and the craftspeople – who put the pattern on it. They placed their whitewashed homes just so in the lee of a hill or planted a shelter of ash trees around the homestead; they founded the hedge banks and built the stone walls that marked out their acres; they and their trade dictated whether the village bar or the market town would survive. They have done so since the indigenous Irish people first began to trade with the invading Celts, and long before the baby St Columba was safely delivered on his Natal Stone by the shores of Lough Akibborn (still a place of pilgrimage for pregnant women seeking a safe birth of their own).

VILLAGE IRELAND

Adare in County Limerick is one of Ireland's prettiest villages; thatched cottages with lime-yellow walls line the wide, main street. Yet Adare, far from having quietly evolved as a typical piece of Irish country life, was brought into being by a nineteenth-century landowner, who landscaped the village to suit his view. Ireland is dotted with planned villages like Adare. A few in southern and eastern Ireland, such as Kilmessan in County Meath, date back to the Normans' habit of founding a cluster of farms and barns around a church. Other villages owe their existence to the craft workers of the past – in the eighteenth century, most of the visitors who arrived at Blarney in County Cork did not come to risk life and limb hanging from the castle battlements to kiss the Blarney stone. Instead they came to admire the prosperous model village of ninety houses, each with its own narrow garden, built to house the families who worked the thirteen local mills. Although the mills closed in the nineteenth century, they later reopened as the Blarney Woollen Mills, which clothed so many soldiers in Blarney tweed during two world wars.

The whitewashed cottages with their shuttered windows and slate-hung walls in Cushendun, County Antrim, were

Like so many dates in the farming calendar, harvest time was a communal affair where families joined forces to help each other. Here neighbouring farmers work together to thresh the corn with a steam-threshing machine.

Co-operation rather than competition was a traditional feature of life in a country that has seen more than its fair share of hardship. Nevertheless, like these two farmers settling a deal by the roadside, country people always enjoyed the business of bargaining.

designed by Clough Williams-Ellis, the architect of Portmeirion in north Wales, and built not to house working weavers but as a Cornish-style memorial to the local landowner's West Country wife. Yet another group of settlements were the chapel villages, established in the early nineteenth century when new Catholic chapels were being built along with a new school, shop and, naturally enough, a public house.

But villages are not a natural feature of the Irish countryside, which is more of a hamlet and township affair with slow roads between. Anonymous-sounding postcodes are not popular and country postal addresses are often vague, personal descriptions like O'Rourke's Place or Reilly's Farm. Visitors are expected to use the reliable local grapevine to find their way around in a place where kinship still holds strong in many of its rural communities. It is not uncommon for a stranger to be greeted by the friendly challenge: 'Now, I know where I'm going, but not where you're coming from.'

When clusters of farmsteads or clachans were formed in country areas, forty or so homesteads would be linked to one another by the complicated network of tracks and little lanes that still patterns the countryside away from the wide, new roads, built more recently with assistance from the European Community. While local people carry a mental map of these old cabbage-leaf motorways, the stranger can expect to lose all sense of direction within a matter of minutes. The habit of haphazard signposting and measuring some distances in miles and other in kilometres all adds to the gentle confusion.

In the old days, the ground around the clachan was worked as rundale. This was a system of dividing the land into manageable strips and plots, which were passed round among the tenants to ensure that everyone had the opportunity to work with both the best and the worst land – exchanges which gave them the alternative name of changedale.

Fifty years before the Great Famine of the 1840s, a population of around eight million put severe pressure on the painful business of scraping a living from the land. Squabbles and arguments over land put a strain on the arrangements, while the practice of dividing the inherited land among all the male heirs of a family subdivided pocket-handkerchief-sized fields into meagre off-cuts. Desperate smallholders planted their traditional lazybeds of potatoes on the bogland margins and spent the early summer using a besom broom to flick a mixture of bluestone and washing soda on to the leaves of the crop to keep disease at bay. But in early June 1845 the sour smell of potato blight was already drifting across the fields and the crop was lost. Blight struck again for the next three years, but by 1846

LEFT

Aran Islanders carry their curragh up the beach. The scene was photographed by the Irish playwright, J. M. Synge, in the early twentieth century during his stay on the islands off the coast of Galway.

ABOVE

In remote and sparsely populated rural areas, the country bar doubles as a grocery store, dispensing beans and bacon with the beer. Such civilized retail arrangements have left many country people with little affection for the busy out-of-town hyperstore or the impersonal supermarket.

famine had begun to bite, and in the next five years famine and fever killed a million people and drove another two and a half million on to the emigration ships.

As labourers and small farmers left or were evicted, their mean turf cottages were pulled down and their farmhouses boarded up, often by agents working for Ireland's absentee landlords. Some of these were landlords who had continued to profit from the rents as their tenants starved. The disaster was at its worst in southern and western Ireland, but the results resounded across the country as, in the shadow of so much poverty, the struggle began to redress the rights of the tenants. Inflated rents, unmanageable mortgages and systematic evictions had made country living intolerable for many working people; the reforms that eventually redistributed almost three-quarters of the land from landowner to tenant were inevitable. Land-reform measures left relatively few of the grand houses with surrounding estates of more 120 hectares (300 acres) or so. As bankrupt owners abandoned their old manor houses, many holdings were reorganized so that the fields formed a convenient series of rectangles spreading out behind the farmhouse, the so-called 'ladder farms' that are still a familiar sight in the Irish countryside. The dispersed farmhouses, each one isolated among its own surrounding fields, were always a particular feature of the Irish landscape; now as farmers and their families emigrated and passed their land on to their neighbour's holdings, rural isolation increased. By the turn of the twentieth century changedale and the clachans had become no more than a folk memory in most parts.

There were psychological as well as physical consequences of all these changes: after the long struggle to own the land they farmed, the families of the new owners cared deeply for the few acres around the old house and were reluctant to part with them. Some teased a modest living from their patch of ground, living frugally and supplementing their income from other sources such as saddle making, thatching or dry stone walling. Some let the land under conacre, a short-term lease; others disappeared without trace, leaving their land and home

'Now, I know where I'm going, but not where you're coming from.'

empty and forlorn in the landscape. Philosophical in the face of adversity, the Irish spirit was not defeated and the farmers' slow and gradual recovery was both kind to the landscape and economical with its resources. Working with hand and hoe spelled survival for the hedgerow and meadow, and this island, which had escaped the worst affects of the Industrial Revolution, retained a clean and relatively unspoiled countryside.

Today there is a fresh spirit of renewal in rural Ireland. For the first time in living memory immigration has exceeded emigration in parts of the west. These days the rising price of property is as likely to be paid by incomers and 'blow-ins' from England, Holland, Germany and America as by the Dublin or Belfast city dweller seeking a new life and home in the Irish countryside. Attracted by the quiet qualities of country life, many of the newcomers are prepared to follow a familiar rural lifestyle with a flock of hens in the backyard, a solid supply of vegetables in the kitchen garden and a milking goat tethered away from the fruit trees in the orchard. These are people who tend to prefer the solid, good looks of the old farmhouse and are sympathetic to preserving those elements of Irish country style that mark their new homes out from the ones they have left behind. It may be no coincidence, but they also tend to have a marked affection for that very Irish institution, the bar.

The pub is still very much a part of Irish country life. More than a mere drinking den, the Irish pub, like the Viennese coffee house or the Parisian café, is a social centre and a trading place for news and gossip. The influence of this archetypal institution has spread far beyond the shores of this island. The tap-room wit and wisdom, the Victorian snug and the pint of dark can now be encountered, somewhat incongruously, anywhere from Montreal to Morocco. But even if the Irish pub has succeeded as a theme place designed to tempt tourists worldwide, it is at its best back home, as any Irish person will tell you. For here, in the quiet country bar, there is no fakery or falsity in the sometimes eccentric collections and ornaments that have accumulated over the decades. The chest of tobacco

drawers, the station clock stopped still at opening time, the 1970 calendar advertising the services of the local undertaker or the naive oil portrait of the hurling team are there because no one has seen the need to move them. And each, if you ask, has a good tale waiting to be told about it – if, that is, you can hear it above the music.

Ireland is the only country in the world to have a musical instrument, the Irish harp, as its national emblem:

> *The harp that once through Tara's halls,*
> *The soul of music shed.*

(THOMAS MOORE 1779–1852)

The harp is capable, say the harpists, of creating laughter, tears and deep dreaming in the right hands, although it is less of a candidate for the bar room than the fiddle or the stretched-skin Irish drum, the *bodhrán*. In the repressive seventeenth century, the melodies of the harp and the rhythmical *bodhrán* were banned because they were suspected of arousing nationalist sentiments. However, you cannot put down a dangerous song and the irrepressible sound of Irish music survived when the players became itinerant musicians and toured their tunes from house to house and inn to inn. Eventually seminal events such as the great harp festival, held in Belfast in 1792, heralded a revival of Irish folk music and helped to bring it back into the musical mainstream. Meanwhile regional music, and the dancing that went with it, developed its own styles and repertoire and thrived in remote rural areas. Now, from the lilting tunes of the blind eighteenth-century harpist, Turlough O'Carolan, to the evocative unaccompanied Irish songs or *sean-nos*, traditional Irish music lives on in country pubs, together with some poetic drinking toasts:

LEFT

The half-empty glass on the bar awaits the singer's return. In the seventeenth century, when public performances of Irish music were banned by the authorities, the ballads and dances survived in the secret drinking dens and shebeens. Today country bars are still the scene of evocative and impromptu performances.

Health and long life to you
The wife (or husband) of your choice to you
A land without rent to you
A child every year to you
And may you be in Heaven for half an hour
Before the Devil knows you're dead.

The twelfth-century Brazen Head which is claimed to be Ireland's oldest pub stands in Dublin, a city which boasts at least eight hundred bars. But, some would say, Dublin is much more famous as the home of the classic pint of Guinness. Arthur Guinness, the world's best-known brewer, established his brewery here in the eighteenth century after experimenting with a beer brewed with roasted barley. It became popular enough with the barrow boys and porters of London's Covent Garden to become their adoptive 'porter'. By the nineteenth century Guinness was brewing nothing but the famous pint of plain. The first export shipments reached Britain in 1769 and by 1820 bottles of Guinness were circumnavigating the world: the novelist Robert Louis Stevenson made sure of his own supplies when he went to the Samoan Islands; and the explorer Douglas Mawson generously left a few bottles at his base camp on the South Pole. By the end of the nineteenth century, the Guinness brewery at Dublin's St James Gate was the largest in the world. Still relying on the same strain of yeast that Arthur Guinness used when he first combined it with Irish grown barley, soft water and hops, the pint of plain seems to have earned the almost universal approval of the Irish (one survey has it that a third of the Irish are teetotal).

If Guinness is the *vin du pays*, then the *eau de vie* is whiskey. Irish monks brought the secrets of distillation back from their devotional journeys to the Holy Lands around AD 600. It was not long before the art of distilling a mixture of malted and unmalted barley, yeast and water was copied by country people in the production of *uisce beatha*, the water of life. The conquering English could not get their tongues around what they clearly enjoyed pouring down their throats and *uisce beatha* was anglicized first into fuisce and finally into whiskey.

The cottage industry produced some fine stuff: Sir Walter Raleigh insisted on taking 32 gallons of *uisce beatha* from the Earl of Cork's home distillery on his voyage to the Americas. Farm distilleries, however, were outlawed by the British government who, while privately recognizing its potential for raising taxable revenues, publicly condemned the consumption of whiskey for its potential to provoke unrest. In the 1830s Father Theobald Mathew's temperance movement had a more formidable effect on country stills when nearly half the adult population signed a pledge of abstinence. But it was the famine of the 1840s that closed down most of the estimated two thousand licensed distilleries and countless secret country stills. By 1900 no more than thirty licensed distilleries survived, Old Bushmills in County Antrim among them. Sir Thomas Phillips, responsible for giving out Ulster's brewery licences in 1608, had issued the first to his own Old Bushmills and it subsequently became the world's oldest licensed distillery. Although few people will admit to it, secret stills which used potatoes to make poteen, the highly alcoholic and illegal spirit, were part of country life within living memory. In her eighties, Mary Redden from County Tyrone could still sing the song:

There's a nice little still at the foot of the hill
With the smoke going up to the sky.
We could easily tell by the woof of the smell
That there's whiskey close by.

The passage of time has done nothing to diminish Irish inventiveness when it comes to alcoholic beverages. The now traditional cup of Irish coffee made with whiskey and cream was the pre-war creation of a barman at Foynes, County Limerick, who devised the drink to sustain passengers on their gruelling twelve-hour transatlantic flight from Foynes to St John, Newfoundland. Memories of such Irish hospitality are partly responsible for Ireland becoming the biggest exporter of liqueurs in the world. Irish cooks too depend on a drop of the good stuff to season their traditional dishes. A whiskey liqueur is regarded as an essential ingredient in colcannon, a dish of cooked potato, kale, leek, butter and cream. Other country dishes include beef braised in Guinness; the County Cork version of black pudding, drisheen; potato cakes, or fadge as they are called in the north, cooked in bacon fat and washed down with hot whiskey and water; and that staple of many an Irish country kitchen, brown soda bread made in a matter of minutes with buttermilk, eggs and stoneground flour. These dishes, like the now renowned Irish cheeses, all originated as country recipes, many of which would have been lost, had it not been for the Irish people's respect for country custom and tradition.

Irish country life, however, is set to change.

Romantic Ireland's dead and gone
It's with O'Leary in the grave,

declared W. B. Yeats, who could not have imagined how his nation's country life was destined to alter under the influence of the twentieth century's global economy and the telecommunications revolution. As the twenty-first century dawns on the Irish countryside, one of the visible benefits, though, of the new age is the number of people returning to work in the countryside.

IRISH HOMEWORK

New technologies have given many people the opportunity to follow a very modern country living. After a long period of disuse, the old outhouses, barns and workshops that once served the country craftspeople are being brought back to life. As the drive to downshift to a quiet country living gathers momentum, more and more homes in the Irish countryside

LEFT
Skeins of home-dyed wool dry on the warming rail of a kitchen cooker. While textile workers always found a place of work at home, a new generation of artists and craftspeople are converting their country homes into studios, workshops and offices.

RIGHT
Changes in farming practices and especially the introduction of Harry Ferguson's mighty little tractor left barns and stables standing empty. Now these redundant country buildings have been given a new lease of life by the Irish renaissance in country crafts.

have been rearranged to accommodate the needs of people who work from home. Tucked in under the beamed ceilings of a converted attic, or settled in to the comfortable confines of a spare bedroom, the country office, equipped with whispering fax machines and winking computer screens, seems light years away from the conventions of traditional country life. Yet the return of these home-based workshops, offices and studios has been less a radical change and more a reversal of fortune for the Irish countryside; Ireland always was home to the homeworker. The new breed of artists, artisans and craftspeople who have chosen a working home with an away-from-it-all feel are only following in the footsteps of generations of wheelwrights, weavers, rope makers, tin smiths, potters and all the other craftspeople who spent long years at their work bench serving their local community.

The two items of furniture that never left the workplace were the chair and the table or bench. From the sacrificial pig bench, used by the butcher when he despatched the farmyard hog, to the fine polished, bog oak office desk, and from the carved-back carpenter's chair to the well-worn horse-hair sofa, country furniture still made an attractive contribution to these workplaces.

A serviceable chair was an essential item of furniture in any studio or workshop. The claims of the antiques dealer to having a set of old 'famine chairs' was treated with caution (since there is little evidence to support the idea that such a thing ever existed). More attractive was the humble hedge chair, turned out by a carpenter with his axe and drawknife from sawmill off-cuts and the occasional knee- or naturally bent piece of hedgerow wood. Since it rarely took a stretcher between its legs, the chair would settle into shape on the traditionally uneven surface of the average Irish kitchen floor. Then there was the three-legged Sligo chair, reproduced for Yeats' tower house at Thoor Ballylee; the Gibson chair of north-east Leinster with its W- or M-shaped spindles on the back rest; and the standard carpenter's chair with its Cupid's bow backrest and curved front legs, made by the dozen – but always by hand – from a single pattern or template hung on the workshop wall.

Buildings suitable for the homeworker range from an artist's studio in a converted barn, flooded with necessary, natural light, to a redundant school room shared by a local collective of homeworkers. From piggeries and potting sheds to barns and byres that have gathered dust in the post-industrial age of the twentieth century, Irish country homes have spawned spare structures suitable for conversion. In the northern and eastern counties, where the old weaver's workroom has been added to one side of the cottage, these workshops have usually been absorbed into the house itself and more likely candidates for conversion are old stables, dairies and milking sheds that have been put out of business by modern agricultural methods. In the southern and western counties, where there is a long-held tradition of building the new house adjacent to the old, some people have been able to restore the old cabin itself to create a suitable workplace.

One man responsible for making more farm buildings redundant than anyone else was Belfast's Harry Ferguson. In the early 1900s when Harry Ferguson was selling tractors imported from America, the horse, ox and donkey reigned supreme. Corn was still sown, cut, carried and even threshed by hand. Firewood and fodder was either transported behind horse- or donkey-drawn vehicles from the basic slide car, a sledge with shafts, to the farm cart, or carried on the smallholder's back with burden ropes made of straw or hay. Baskets of turf or laundry were carried on the head, cushioned by a ring of hay, the *fáinne*. In those days every animal needed its stable, every crop its store house, every farm implement its shed and every craft its workshop.

When Harry Ferguson's first tractor rolled off the assembly lines at Coventry in England, it rumbled towards a total transformation of farming in Ireland. Although it was said to attract the amorous attentions of the farm bull, Harry Ferguson's tractor was, at first, mocked for its ugly looks and derided for its cost. But it turned out to be a mighty little monster as happy hauling peat or potatoes as it was carrying the family, balanced on the mudguards, to church and school. Within a couple of decades the barn, the byre, the cart and the wagon shed had fallen into disuse.

Now as these redundant buildings take on a new lease of life, the homeworkers who occupy them, many of them craftspeople, are helping to preserve the best of Irish country life.

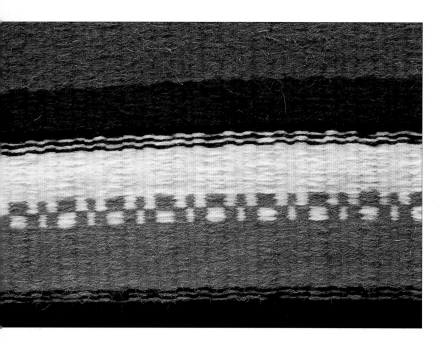

'Every article … has an almost personal character which gives this simple life, where all art is unknown, something of the beauty of medieval life.'

Irish Crafts

From the hand craft of the weaver, above, to the art of the thatcher, opposite, the products of Ireland's craftspeople have an ancient past and a promising future. Once the craftspeople furnished the homes of their local communities. Now there is an international market for Irish crafts.

LADDERBACK CHAIRS AND HAND-STITCHED QUILTS; simple oak sideboards and pictures of pressed flowers; plank-top tables and wickerwork peat baskets – the handmade crafts of Ireland are an integral part of its country style.

From the linen mills of Lagan to the marble workshops of Connemara, Ireland's crafts are developing into a major industry. Outlets range from the craft villages of the west, where groups of artisans have joined forces to make and market their wares, to the small potter's studio or jeweller's workshop hidden away in the depths of the countryside. They are following in that noble tradition described by J. M. Synge as he photographed the rope makers and spinners of the Aran Islands. 'Every article on these islands has an almost personal character which gives this simple life, where all art is unknown, something of the artistic beauty of medieval life.'

The work of the Irish craftspeople has a long and honourable past, which has encompassed everything from the Georgian silversmith's classic three-legged sugar bowls to the utilitarian willow-stick creels and rush-work baskets of the country housewife. There is the *Book of Kells*, that extraordinarily beautiful manuscript, illuminated in the eighth century, and currently held in the Old Library of Trinity College, Dublin. There were the 149 volumes of manuscript journals, described by one observer as 'probably the most majestic series of bound volumes in the world', covered in crimson morocco and elaborately tooled by Irish bookbinders in the

eighteenth century. They were all destroyed by fire in 1922. Still in the eighteenth century there were the stylized mahogany side tables and cabinets, intricately carved with foliage, grotesque faces and animal heads by cabinet makers who, a century later, were turning their attention to bog-oak ornaments and furniture, inlaid with convoluted Celtic motifs such as the shamrock and the wolfhound.

More than two thousand grand Palladian and neo-classical manor houses still stood dotted around the countryside at the turn of the twentieth century and most of them harboured some example of the Irish crafts. Despite the assertion of some (usually English) critics that the Irish builder was hopelessly inept – 'In this country they have not the art of building a staircase,' maintained one English clergyman – the Georgian inheritance itself was the work of a multitude of Irish artisans from stonecutters, glaziers, wire workers and bricklayers, to carpenters, sawyers, joiners and cabinet makers. (The fine plaster work of many a Georgian ceiling was attributed to Italian workmanship until it was discovered that Robert West and Michael Stapelton, Ireland's own two master stuccodores – from the Italian *stuccatore* or plaster worker – were responsible for much

of the work.) Irish craftsmanship, of course, was not confined to indulging the whims of the rich and wealthy; it was also a fundamental part of the life of every country community. If a donkey lost a shoe or a plough broke a blade, its owner approached the local blacksmith; if the farmer needed a new press for the parlour or his wife wanted a new pine top to put on her kitchen table, they called on the local cabinet maker or joiner. The relationship between the craftsperson and his or her community was one of mutual benefit; but it was a relationship which was doomed to come to an end with the advent of the Industrial Revolution and mass production.

Under the rejuvenating influence of the Arts and Crafts movement, the closing decades of the nineteenth century saw a reaction against the cheap products of the factory-line, and the new millennium of the twentieth century heralded a brief, but significant revival of crafts such as hand-weaving, embroidery and jewellery. Irish craftspeople has continued to produce outstanding work throughout this century, although the number of craftspeople have inevitably declined. 'Half a century ago, [the work of the craftsman] was not esteemed by the new middle class when they came to homemaking,' explained Justin

*T*he Irish carvers and cabinet makers of the eighteenth century developed a vigorous and unmistakable style, leaving their distinctive hallmark on pieces such as this ornate mahogany card table. Having replaced the homegrown oak with timber traded from the West Indies, they embellished it with fantastic faces and curling foliage.

*T*he Temple of the Winds at Newtownards in County Down was built as a banqueting pavilion for Mount Stewart House by James Stuart in the late eighteenth century. Its exquisite inlaid floor and plasterwork are as spectacular as its views across Strangford Lough.

Keating, chairman of the Craft Council of Ireland in the 1980s. 'The imported and mass produced was chic. The indigenous, the traditional, the work of the craftsman was neglected.'

One of the great tragedies has been the gradual disappearance of the Irish stonecutters. Their work spans more than thirteen centuries and it is difficult to find a place in Ireland where their handiwork has not made its mark. It is there in the churchyards' high crosses with their complex carvings of scriptural tales; the sculpted stone mullions, chimney-breasts and ogee-arched doorways of the old abbeys and castles; the Gallarus Oratory in County Kelly, a stone house jigsaw built

has come too late; they and their skills have mostly disappeared.

Elsewhere, there are signs of a significant resurgence in Irish craft work, partly in response to a number of government and private schemes designed to foster and encourage the traditional crafts. Perhaps this renewed interest is also because, in this disorientating world of mass production, we still want what Justin Keating described as 'the reassurance of living with objects which are quite clearly the work of one particular identifiable individual person, working in a particular place, on a particular day, and within a particular tradition'.

The laceworkers' expertise was brought to Ireland from southern Europe in the nineteenth century, but nimble fingers were soon producing work with a distinctive Irish flavour such as the distinctive rose motif of Clones, County Monaghan on this wedding dress.

Pieces like this delicate appliqué lace collar were beyond the reach of the woman who spent long hours making it. A product of the lace schools in Carrickmacross, County Monaghan, the lace was sold to supplement low incomes.

entirely without mortar; even the humble kerb stones, once fashioned by hand and cold chisel.

A small army of artisans used to be involved in handling the stone. There were the quarry men who removed the stone and the stonecutters who roughly shaped it, the masons who built with it and the carvers who gave it its final, freestyle form. These were the men who turned slabs of Liscannor slate into fireplaces and mantelpieces, and cut Moher stone into roof slates and flagstones. Now, the growing demand for their services to help with the restoration of old homes and gardens

LACE

Until the Industrial Revolution, craft work was the lifeblood of many rural communities and the few pence earned by hand-stitching lace collars late into the evening could make the difference between survival and starvation.

The oldest of the lace industries, Carrickmacross in County Monaghan, arose as a result of the local rector's honeymoon in the nineteenth century. When the Reverend and Mrs Porter took their nuptial holiday in Italy, the good Reverend's wife learned the craft of embroidered lace making from the

Italians and taught the skills to local women on her return. Now the Sisters of St Louis Convent support a labour-intensive lace makers' co-operative whose distinctive swans, flowers, harps and shamrocks have become collectors' items. Another rector's wife introduced lace making in Clones, County Monaghan, and the distinctive raised Clones knot is still a feature of modern lace work there. Just as the Providence Woollen Mills at Foxford, County Mayo, was founded in 1892 by the Reverend Mother Agnes Morrogh Bernard to try to stem the flow of emigrants, so the lace makers of Kenmare in County Kerry were set up by local nuns for famine relief.

Four Irish nuns, who travelled to Paris in 1769 to learn the craft and returned to teach it to the poor families of Cork, originally introduced the high-quality hand-crochet lace so sought after by fashion designers today. Much of the early Irish lace work stemmed from projects designed to give the poor, who could not afford to wear it, the chance at least to earn an income from it. Lace schools where flounces, handkerchiefs, collars and lengths of lace braid were diligently stitched by the womenfolk were a common feature of rural life and nineteenth-century Irish lace, renowned for its fine qualities, has become a cherished collectible.

The oldest form of lace making was bobbin or pillow lace. A design was pricked out on parchment fixed to a pad. The threads, wound on a bobbin, were painstakingly plaited around pins that marked out the design. With tatting, an ivory shuttle was passed through a series of handmade loops and knots of thread.

Long after Queen Victoria graciously accepted the gift of a Kenmare lace collar in 1881, the decorative qualities of Irish lace have been regularly used to put the finishing touches to country windows and walls.

LINEN

As famous as Irish lace, Irish linen is renowned for its durability and quality. Once widespread throughout Ulster and neighbouring Connaught, linen making began life as a cottage industry, but with the arrival of Huguenot refugees from France became a fully fledged industry in the Lagan Valley of Counties Down and Antrim. One of the Huguenots, Louis Cromelin, was asked by the English king to improve and expand the local linen industry: he did so with such success that by the nineteenth century the weaving centre at Lisburn was producing half the nation's linen. As Belfast turned into the linen centre of the world, almost a quarter of a million acres of land were devoted to growing the industry's basic material, the pretty, blue-flowered flax.

Flax was pulled up by the roots when it was ready, then 'retted' or soaked in water until, it was said, the smell became unbearable. Before men such as the Scottish settler John Barbour helped to mechanize the linen industry, it was the cottagers who would dry, spin and weave the flax and, when it had been bleached, embroider or 'flower' the cloth to give it a distinctive Irish finish.

While the modern manufacturers now import most of their flax, the quality and durability of Irish-made linen has assured it a place in Irish country homes. Irish linen cloth is also exported to the fashion houses of Japan and Italy and used by Ireland's own fashion industry. Double damask table linen and hand-embroidered linen sheets from County Donegal are still on sale in Ulster's linen shops.

TEXTILE CRAFTS

The Aran islanders, hardy men and women who wrested a living from the windswept chain of islands off the Galway coast, always supplemented their farming and fishing income with textile crafts, knitting and weaving with homespun wool. Their stitching developed a vocabulary of its own and, since the stitching and cabling varied from community to community, the place of origin of some poor drowned sailor could be traced from the stitch of his sweater. While trellis stitch

RIGHT

Linen making in Ireland started as a cottage craft, but by the nineteenth century had developed into a major industry in Ulster. The manufacture of Aran sweaters centre, however, has remained essentially a cottage industry.

mirrored the pattern of the stonewalled fields on the islands, cable stitch was said to represent the islanders' fishing ropes and diamond stitch its fishing nets. There was a trinity or blackberry stitch, a pattern of three points in one representing the Christian triumvirate; double zigzag stitch to represent the ups and downs of married life; and moss stitch as a symbol of wealth. Honeycomb stitch was a symbol of good luck – sighting a swarm of bees before setting out to sea was thought to be an auspicious omen.

When J. M. Synge stayed on the islands in the early days of the twentieth century, he was given a pair of traditional shoes or pampooties which in his words 'consisted simply of a piece of raw cowskin, with the hair outside, laced over the toe and round the heel with two ends of fishing line that work round and are tied above the instep'. The islanders placed the pampooties in a bowl of water at night to keep the leather supple. The island men wore a crios, a woven woollen belt that car-

ried bold dashes of bright-coloured wool between its clean, white edges and was made by stringing the warp threads between hand and foot rather than on a loom.

Irish weavers have been turning sheep's wool into cloth for at least nine centuries. Even when overseas markets for Irish-worked wool declined, the weavers continued to meet the local demand for the light woollen cloth, flannel, used to make shifts and shirts, and tweed, the hard-wearing cloth that went into the making of coats and trousers. It was an arduous process. The fleece was sheared in one piece from the sheep, carded to straighten the fibres of wool and separate them from the fleece, and then spun on the spinning wheel to produce the lengths of yarn ready for dyeing and weaving. Traditional hand-woven tweed is still made in country places like County Donegal where newcomers have helped to breathe fresh life into the old craft, rejuvenating traditional techniques with contemporary colours and designs. Knitters still form the biggest group of working

LEFT
Two Aran island women pose by their spinning wheel for a photograph by J. M. Synge in the early 1900s.

craftspeople in Ireland today, painstakingly producing work of a quality impossible to replicate by industrial methods.

County Donegal's hand-knitted carpets, made at Killybegs after the founding of a factory there in 1898 by a Scotsman, Alexander Morton, were another high-demand craft product. Individually designed and handmade from 100 per cent wool, the carpets went to cushion the feet of, amongst others, passengers on the *Queen Mary* and visitors to Buckingham Palace.

Yet another textile craft which has undergone a remarkable

revival is the patchwork quilt. Having been introduced to Ireland by the English aristocracy, and spread down the social scale and across the country from east to west, patchwork quilting always provided a useful excuse for village women to get together. It reached a highpoint in the 1850s, but the art of quilt making nearly died out in the 1920s. However, its late-twentieth-century revival by professional designer craft workers has transformed the craft into a highly creative art form.

Traditional patchwork quilts, made of a top, back and an

OPPOSITE PAGE

From handmade Donegal carpets to homemade shawls and blankets, the fruits of the Irish loom have given this country's crafts a reputation for good looks and fine quality.

THIS PAGE

The work of the weavers is an essential element of Irish country style whether it is the close colours of a textile weave, right, *the classic tweeds of the Avoca handweavers in County Wicklow,* below, *or a contemporary weaving,* below right.

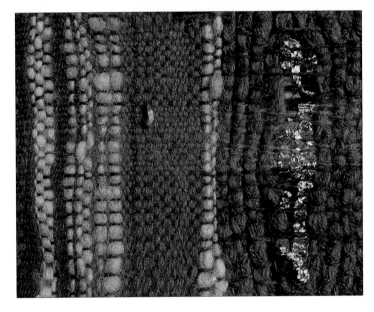

interlining for extra comfort, ranged from a functional piece of bedding to intricately woven show quilts destined for the marriage bed or the provident bottom drawer. While the better off in society could recycle their old gowns and dresses, poorer people would buy scraps of cloth since their own clothes were too well-worn to be used. These materials – leftovers from the dressmaker's visit, redundant military uniforms, flour sacks, even tailor's sample books – give an insight into the social lives of the quilters, who would sit and stitch, six or eight women together, as busy matchmaking their sons and daughters as they were with their sewing needles.

There were various quilting techniques. In the appliqué method, fabrics were sewn directly on to cotton or calico. Those who could not afford to buy their cotton opened old flour sacks, bleached them clean and then sewed them together to make the quilt back; the faint lines of the flour company's trademarks can still be seen in some rare samples. With the mosaic method, geometric shapes were sewn together, the wealthier women using expensive paper templates to create their patchworks. The log cabin method, more commonly known as folded work, involved sewing strips of light and dark material around a central square. This method may have originated in the back room of some Connemara farmhouse, although no such samples have survived; alternatively the log cabin technique, which was also popular in America, may have come from emigrant families sending patterns back home to their families and friends in Ireland.

Regional quilters had their preferred colours and patterns: for example, turkey red, a cheap dyed cotton, and white, freely available from old flour sacks, was a common choice among Ulster women. Precious old quilts like these are sometimes used as wall hangings in contemporary country homes.

CHINA

Waiting for her quilting party to arrive, a hostess might prepare a little light refreshment, setting it out on her best porcelain. From the late seventeenth century, pottery centres in Belfast, Dublin, Limerick, Rostrevor and Youghal kept the household stocked with their delft or tin-glazed earthenware. When the English firm of Wedgwood perfected its white earthenware in

BELOW

Best Belleek china took pride of place in the nineteenth-century Irish parlour. Made by hand at the pottery in County Fermanagh, pieces like this nineteenth-century shell-shaped jelly dish, below left, *or the early-twentieth-century oval basket,* below right, *have become collectors' items.*

the 1760s, Irish potters at Belfast and Doneraile in County Cork used the same techniques for their own creamware. But Belleek, with its fine, mother-of-pearl-like finish and delicate plant-like forms, was judged the finest. It was in 1857 that John Caldwell Bloomfield brought together the felspar, kaolin, flint, clay, schist and turf necessary to make the translucent, creamy porcelain that eventually made Belleek in County Fermanagh a household name. After a period of earthenware production, the Belleek pottery works began producing porcelain, the workers, their hands greased with olive oil, weaving strands of clay mixed with gum arabic into fine, fragile porcelain baskets,

LEFT

The fluid form of an early-nineteenth-century chandelier hangs framed by a window in Waterford Town Hall. The Waterford crystal factory reopened in the 1950s after going bankrupt in 1851.

BELOW

A set of courtly, club-shaped decanters, made in Cork in the nineteenth century, demonstrates the style and quality of Irish glass. The art of hand-blown glass has been revitalized by contemporary craftspeople such as Keith Leadbetter at Jerpoint Glass Studios in Kilkenny.

tureens, cups and saucers, which were destined to join the proud country housewife's collection.

Another clay product was the dudeen or clay pipe, produced by the thousand until affordable, ready-rolled cigarettes put the pipe maker out of business. Clay pipes used to play a prominent part in everyday life. They were given away free with beer, distributed at wakes and even ceremoniously placed on the graves of the dear departed. Pipes were sometimes filled with sponc, an aromatic mix of coltsfoot and herbs smoked as an alternative to expensive tobacco, and produced in different designs with evocative names such as the Cavehill Cutty, the Shamrock, the Lily and the Johnston of Ballykilbeg.

In the eighteenth century, the country potter's craft, which dates back at least six thousand years, was concentrated on the production of the great glazed earthenware crocks for storing milk and shallow dishes for souring cream. By the mid-nineteenth century local potteries were as likely to be turning their skills to tile and brick making as they were producing fashionable kitchenware on a hand-turned potter's wheel. Cottage potteries turned the Irish clay into a whole range of household items: cowls for the chimney, bowls for flower bulbs, pots for parsley, mugs for beer, jugs for water, holders for candles and money boxes for souvenirs. Since the 1950s Irish studio potters like Peter Brennan have been responsible for bringing fine table and ornamental pottery into the public domain. These days, when other studio potters such as the respected ceramic artist Maxine Mearns of County Limerick return the local pottery to the Irish craft scene, no household is complete without its set of pottery mugs and no garden without its terracotta pots.

GLASS

Glass was being made in Ireland even before the Celts began turning out their chunks of decorative stones formed from fused glass rods. Until its decline in the nineteenth century, the glass-making centres around Belfast, Dublin, Waterford and Cork turned potash, bright white silica sand and red lead oxide into delicate vases, candelabra, jugs, window panes and drinking glasses. Now Ireland is better known for its lead crystal glass, made world-famous by a little glass-making business set up at Waterford in 1783. Two brothers, George and William

Penrose, founded the glass works to create glass with the 'character and purity of pure crystal', but even as they were being awarded prestigious gold medals at London's Great Exhibition of 1851, the business was bankrupt. In the 1940s, crystal glass makers resurrected the secret formula for Waterford glass. Once again the furnaces were fired up and the Waterford workers began to turn out their deeply etched, hand-blown glass.

Contemporary craftspeople who produce handmade studio glassware have also contributed to Ireland's reputation for fine glass. Keith Leadbetter, for example, after travelling Europe to master the skills of working hot glass, established a studio near Jerpoint Abbey in 1979. Now a group of glass makers at the Jerpoint Studio produce their handmade pieces, each with its tell-tale base mark from the puntil iron, the iron that holds the glass while the rim is finished by hand, after it has been separated from its blowing iron. From fluted bowls to butter dishes, and from sparkling decanters to paperweights, all may find a place in the Irish home.

BASKET MAKING

'Down by the salley garden my love and I did meet,' wrote W. B. Yeats at the turn of the twentieth century when the craft of basket making and willow work was a skill familiar to almost any country person with a strong pair of hands and a patch of ground where they could grow their willow or sally. Old enough to lay claim to being the mother craft of pottery, basketry certainly served as an acceptable substitute for china dishes or bowls well into the twentieth century as families sat down to share their meal of potatoes from the skib (from the Irish *sciob*). Like almost every kind of basket, the skib, a shallow wickerwork tray in which the cooked potatoes were served, had various regional names including a scuttle (County Clare), a *ciseóg* (County Galway) and the poetic sally saucer (County Louth). Around the farmhouse, creative basketry fulfilled every conceivable purpose from a dog's muzzle to a baby's rattle while the most basic basket, the creel or *cliabhh*, was a burden basket, made to suit any purpose from a donkey's pannier to a fisherman's backpack. There were two different forms of basket making: the sturdy, everyday items such as eel traps and log baskets; and the fancy, decorative basket work such

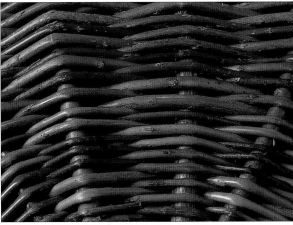

The twisted weave of willow creates a perfect pattern. The basket maker and his sally or willow field have been part of the Irish scene since time immemorial. Now basket makers from home and abroad come to learn the traditional skills from master craftsmen like Joe Hogan in County Galway, pictured here cutting his willows.

as the baby's crib or Moses basket. Most of the professional basket makers were once concentrated in two regions, around the shores of Lough Neagh in the north, and in the Suir Valley in Munster, but after centuries of settled work, commercial basketry became a notoriously capricious market. When, for example, front lights were made compulsory for bicycles, the market for bicycle baskets was dealt a death blow. And when cardboard boxes were introduced they spelled the end of the wickerwork railway hampers, herring crans, potato skeps, flower baskets and skips, in which commercial travellers carried their wares from town to town. Now basketry has become another Irish craft that has undergone a resurgence, not only to meet modern demands for anything from wicker seats to

hot-air balloon baskets, but also because so many people want to learn what is one of the oldest traditional crafts.

Along with the export of its most portable cultural possessions – its words and its music – Irish crafts, from Waterford crystal to Donegal tweed, continue to find a ready market overseas. Coopers and furniture makers, boat builders and clog makers, bowl turners and *bodhrán* makers have been joined by basket makers, candle makers, willow workers and jewellers to meet the demand for Irish crafts. But the products of keen eyes and dextrous fingers will always find a place in the Irish home and anything from a Connemara wall hanging to a medieval-style Kerry tile has a part to play in contemporary Irish country style.

*'Full of beauty and distinction' where
'the walls have been turned by turf-smoke to
a soft brown that blends with the grey earth-
colour of the floor'.*

Irish Kitchens
and Parlours

*There is an understandable passion for
porches, right, in a country where the annual
rainfall could be described as generous.
From the modest porch hood to a structure
the size of an extra room, the porch, like
the fanlight above, is a traditional feature
of Irish homes.*

STEP THROUGH THE GATE and into the gentle greenery of the Irish cottage garden and you enter a world where the pace of life seems strangely unhurried and where there is a distinct lack of enthusiasm for change. Down the decades these country kitchens and living rooms have changed, but not beyond recognition: their country colours, fabrics and furniture have contributed to a finish that still owes its ancestry to the traditional elements of Irish country style.

HALLS AND PORCHES

Despite the differences that gave the provinces their distinctive character, there is a curious homogeneity to Irish country homes. The dictates of this mild, damp climate and the disposition of a highly sociable people led to some common conventions. The solid porch, the communal kitchen, the civilized parlour and that conversation piece of kitchen furniture, the Irish country dresser, its shelves brimming with best china, were to be found all the way from Cork to Cookstown.

The porch was a particular example of Irish style encountered on homes new and old. An essential feature in a country which meets the wet westerly winds of the Atlantic, the porch might be translated into a simple hood or a pair of sheltering

Creating a classic entry to the Georgian country box house, the porch or portico was a fashionable addition with an entirely practical purpose – it was spacious enough to shelter an entire family as they waited for the maid.

RIGHT

This Georgian hall in County Wexford is flooded with natural daylight from windows on either side of the door and the fanlight above. Pale walls lighten the room and a pot overflowing with flowers adds a welcoming touch.

ABOVE

A door on a perfectly proportioned house in County Derry is flanked by symmetrical windows and framed with clean-cut stone. A door that is out of character will alter the look of the whole house.

walls outside the front door of a small market-town house. Once a useful place to hang a brace of hare for the pot, these days it is more likely to harbour a set of tinkling wind chimes or a hanging flower basket.

In rural areas the porch was more often a solid and sometimes incongruous addition to whitewashed cabins and brick bungalows alike. Contemporary porches, like their predecessors, might be lit by a pair of windows on either side and simply furnished with a stone bench, where older family members could enjoy the afternoon sun and keep a gossip's eye on the comings and goings in the lane outside. The porch presented an irresistible opportunity for display – a scented geranium grown in a cracked teapot, a candle lantern over the pendant porch light, a piece of sea-weathered driftwood hung against the wall. In days gone by these would have kept company with the ash-handled turf cutter, the potato fork and the scythe, old tools which some discerning gardeners have now rescued, restored and turned into collectors' items.

An outside door often closed off the porch on the smaller cottages and cabins of the west, turning the room into a modest hall equipped with a wet-weather floor and plenty of raincoat pegs and boot racks. Elsewhere, on larger homes, the hall opened off the porch, perhaps lit by a Georgian-style fanlight or at least a good copy – one resourceful antiques dealer formed hers from a pair of coathangers and was delighted to find it later praised as the genuine article. Another favourite Irish design was the semi-circular Diocletian window which, with its two flanking windows, was often used to light a central staircase.

Pale colourwashes which were carried up across the ceiling to reflect the light into the hall, simple flagstone or quarry-tile floors, and the odd piece of furniture – a limewashed country chair or a fine old terracotta pot – all made a welcoming experience of that transition from outdoors to indoors. In the absence of a window to light the hall, a half-glazed door, perhaps veiled with a little muslin for privacy, served the same purpose. The outside door was a key element in the look of any house and a fussy or heavily ornamented door did a disservice to the small, or cottage-style, house. The salvaged, repaired and repainted door was preferable to a new door, which was usually more expensive and less well made. In parts of Ireland where the house was built of exposed stone, the old practice of highlighting the door frame in whitewash allowed the door itself to take a contrasting, bright, bold colour. Where the rest of the house was whitewashed, and dressed stones such as granite were used to frame the doorway, the stones were traditionally kept free of paint.

IRISH KITCHENS

In the elegant old farmhouse the hall led to the parlour door, but in the cottage it passed straight into that heart of the home, the kitchen. J. M. Synge described such a kitchen with its earth floors and open rafters as a place 'full of beauty and distinction' where 'the walls have been turned by turf-smoke to a soft brown that blends with the grey earth-colour of the floor'. After a polite period when the kitchen was placed out of bounds to visitors, who reluctantly let themselves be led into the chilly parlour, the kitchen resumed its status as the centrepoint of the house. Whether it stood in the straw-thatched bungalows of coastal County Wexford or in the windswept western farmhouses of Connemara, the Irish kitchen contained many of the elements typical of country life. There might be a set of *súgáns* or rope-seated chairs, an open-frame pine settle, the lines of its bottle-green panels perhaps picked out in yellow paint, or a creepie, that low, three-legged stool whose origins lie in the not-so-distant past when, in the chimneyless house, fumes from the peat fire hung in a head-high pall of smoke.

'[They] vent their smoak like those of the Hottentots,' reported one astonished eyewitness. Now bright enamelled stoves have mostly replaced the open fires on which a slow pot cooked the midday meal, but the fondness for the heat of peat remains and many of the modern multi-fuel stoves are designed to burn peat as well as logs and coal.

LEFT

This kitchen in County Wicklow is filled with features from the past: the toasting fork and salt box, the shelf over the fire with its spit rack or cleevy, and a pine settle which could be opened out at night to provide extra sleeping space for guests.

OPPOSITE PAGE

Under a pine-panelled ceiling, a contemporary kitchen draws on elements of its Irish past. A wickerwork potato skip serves a more decorative than practical purpose while the bandy-legged milking stool, rescued from the old dairy, finds a new place of rest beside the house stove.

KITCHEN DRESSER

Along with the stove, the kitchen dresser has always been a universally popular part of the kitchen. Preyed upon by antiques dealers and threatened by cheap imitations, the Irish dresser has nevertheless survived for at least four centuries. Unlike its Celtic counterpart, the two-piece Welsh dresser, Irish dressers were made in one piece, the top half of open shelves and the bottom half of drawers, shelves and occasionally chicken coops. The old business of keeping a couple of laying hens clucking away in the corner of the kitchen has become a joke which Irish country people tell against themselves, but the cottager who had a ready supply of eggs through the winter enjoyed the last laugh. These days the hens have been banished to their proper quarters at the end of the garden and, on the dresser, panelled doors or open shelves sheltering behind a cotton curtain have taken their place.

The upper shelves of the dresser were designed to display the household china – a favourite collection of Belleek porcelain or, in the case of one housewife from Antrim, the Delftware she had recovered from a shipwreck. Like other furniture in the Irish home, the dresser was painted, sometimes in two tones, with the lighter tone such as cream, yellow or white used on the boards behind the upper shelves to backlight the crockery. The custom of painting the dresser may be making a slow comeback, but the carpenter's habit of lavishing decorative details on the woodwork never went away. Uprights carved with elaborate spirals, Celtic interlacing, classical pilasters and fascia boards shaped like the curves of a fiddle or cupid's bows and pierced with shamrocks, hearts or diamonds have traditionally featured on the Irish dresser.

Then as now the dresser and its display were there to be admired. Plate was stood on its side and leaned on removable bars so that the firelight caught the patterns. Basins or bowls were whammelled or turned upside down and piled in a pyramid to show off their decoration, and prized silver spoons lined the top shelves, sometimes set in special slots cut out for that purpose. One or two of the best pieces of china might no longer be usable following a fall, but since they remained as pretty as the day they were bought at market they continued to be kept on display.

Some country people can recall the time when the broad board of the faithful farmhouse dresser fulfilled a very special function – it was where the corpse would be respectfully laid out following a death in the family. The everyday purpose of the dresser's wide front shelf was for preparing or dressing the food, a role that has been superseded by modern wood, stone or tiled worktops.

These days the most highly prized dressers are those miniatures that were made by craftsmen to advertise their skills and expertise, but in the 1930s it was the glass-fronted dressers that fetched the best prices. Adding glazed doors to the old kitchen dresser was a reasonable excuse for asking appreciative neighbours over, since the country dresser always was, and always will be, a source of pride and a measure of social status. The well-heeled farmer could expect to dig deep into his purse to pay for his, while the poor cottager might have to rely on barter – a stout beef bullock was reckoned to be a reasonable price.

Dressers were typically stood facing the hearth, the better to reflect the firelight – unlike the settle, which stood beside the fire, where its high back kept away the draughts. At nightfall the base of the settle slid out to form a bed where, cushioned by a soft feather or raw straw mattress, the household children could sleep soundly by the fire.

The cottage dresser often stood on an earth floor, but was none the worse for it since the floor was naturally sealed with something such as skimmed milk or animal blood and polished until it shone. In northern and western Ireland especially, the dresser was fitted with a distinctive sledge foot or boot dovetailed into the base for stability. When the worn boots gave way a new set of feet were fitted and the dresser was good for another decade or two. Times change. Many an old country dresser has been adapted to hold the television set while many more have had these projecting boots removed, partly because there is no danger of them rotting away on the contemporary tile or timber floor and partly because they get in the way of the broom. It is a sad loss, since the sledge foot is a distinctly Irish feature and one that has helped to establish the provenance of 'the auld dresser' as far away as Australia. For the Irish people carried their customs, traditions and furniture designs

ABOVE

Irish dressers were painted to conceal the mixed provenance of their timbers. This one in County Tyrone stands by a sliding sash window, the better to light its collection of plate and bowls and the rush cross woven for the feast of Saint Brigid.

to every corner of the globe – for example, the direct descendant of the Californian Murphy bed was the Irish press bed, while many an American and Canadian country settle has its roots in the Irish kitchen.

KITCHEN FURNITURE

When Irish emigrants settled the New World they welcomed the abundant supplies of fresh wood to build their country furniture. It made a rare change from the homeland where the country carpenter was known as the hedge carpenter because it was from here that he was compelled to find much of his wood. Most Irish dressers, settles and other household items were made from cheap matchboarding imported from Spain, the Baltics and the British mainland.

Repairs were often carried out in rescued wood. Ironically

In small country homes the kitchen continues to be the place where meals are prepared and served and where the family gathers in the evening. Here familiar features such as the ceramic sink and the 1930s glazed-top dresser are combined with floral stencils and limewashed walls to create an eyecatching finish.

LEFT

'The kitchen was the very heart of the traditional Irish home and its hearth-fire was the focal point, drawing visitors to it like a magnet.' In larger country homes, the old kitchen with its solid sideboard, flagstone floors and inglenook fireplace is once again at the heart of the home.

one source of recycled furniture wood was directly associated with the ebb of Ireland's lifeblood. Furniture makers in the mid-nineteenth century made small domestic pieces like plate racks, stepped spoon racks and eggs boxes from the short staves used as packing material between the barrels of flax seed imported by sailing ship from America. It was the masters of these same boats who looked for a cargo to fill their empty holds on the return trip and turned to the trade in people, filling their coffin ships with Irish emigrants.

Along the Irish coast, wood from a shipwreck or a cargo lost overboard in a storm inevitably found its way into house and home. When the steamship Asian struck Stag Rock and sank off the west coast of Cork in 1924, country carpenters in the area were briefly rewarded with a rich crop of fresh timber. Chairs, settle backs, dressers and press beds received a new lease of life as flotsam from the stricken vessel drifted ashore. Harvested from the beaches by local villagers, the deal boards and mahogany covers were pressed into service to repair the old furniture and create new pieces.

Carpenters carefully concealed any sea damage, keeping scarred surfaces on the inside or the underside of the furniture, or filling in and painting over any holes. Stripping the paint from a piece of furniture may reveal these ancient sea marks, but it does not restore country pieces to their original state since people painted all but their best furniture to preserve the wood and hide the effect of using several types of wood on one item. The few pieces, that were untouched by a paintbrush are waxed or varnished today, whereas in the past they would be regularly scrubbed and scoured until the bare wood gleamed.

STORAGE

If the Irish people were short of homegrown wood, they were also short of space. Dual-purpose furniture like the settle bed helped, as did the folding breakfast table which made

The kitchen was the very heart of the traditional Irish home and its hearth-fire was the focal point, drawing visitors to it like a magnet.

its way with the Irish emigrants from the country kitchens of the old home to the chic apartments of New York's Manhattan. The let-down, or falling table as it was known, was common throughout rural Ireland at the turn of the twentieth century. So too were the drop-down tables that doubled as cupboard doors, tables with tops with a hole in one end which could be hung on the wall, tables that folded out from the back of the settle and tables attached to a length of iron railing set into the wall, which were moved close to or away from the fire according to the season.

Some tables had egg holes cut in them, one for each place at the table, which dispensed with the need for egg cups. Even the most fragile-looking table was expected to service a variety of needs, from cutting up the barrow pig (the largest in the litter, traditionally killed at Michaelmas in September) to giving work space to the journeyman tailor, who would sit cross-legged on its board, working by the light of the window.

Old habits die hard. The modern practice of positioning the kitchen sink beneath the window is still resisted by traditionalists, who prefer to put the kitchen table there instead. People who saw no good reason to be rid of their heavy stone, Belfast sinks when their neighbours were replacing theirs with stainless steel now find the Belfast sink returning to favour in fashionable kitchens. Although mains electricity has reached all but the remotest rural communities, the flickering friendliness of candle- and lamplight has persisted. Candles set in cast-iron wall holders and sconces backed by a piece of reflective tin still cast a warming light on an evening gathering; paraffin lamps and storm lanterns have been brought back into service as lamp shades while the *coinneal mór*, the great red candle, still makes its traditional appearance at the kitchen window on Christmas Eve.

One lighting solution unlikely to return to favour is the ancient crusie lamp. The crusie was a pair of pear-shaped metal vessels, one set above the other. A wick made from a strip of twisted lint lay dipped in the oil-filled upper vessel, dripping spent fuel into the one below. When fish oil was the only fuel available the crusie had to be hung as close to the hearth as possible so that the foul smell of burning oil was wafted away up the chimney.

Also long gone from most country hearths are the cooking cranes, sometimes of iron, sometimes solid bog oak, which swung over the fire and from which an assortment of pots,

griddles, skillets and kettles were suspended. However, traditional cookware has not disappeared completely. Even in this age of non-stick kitchen equipment the favourite family copper kettle still bubbles on the hob although the smoke-blackened, three-legged cauldron is more likely to have been relegated to the garden and filled with flowers.

The character of the Irish kitchen came from its being composed of individual pieces of furniture, robust, well worn and always preferable to the monotonous effect of mass-produced units. There were wooden meal arks for storing flour and corn, and slatted racks hung from the rafters for keeping sides of salted meat, but now holding bunches of fresh herbs or dried flowers. Wall and corner cupboards, open pine shelves, towel rails and peg rails all provided convenient storage and house-

BELOW

Odd shelves and old wall cabinets provide storage space in a creative country kitchen. The quintessential character of the Irish kitchen came from its mix and match of furniture and fittings rather than the use of standard units and fixtures.

wives devised a resourceful range of 'tidies' for keeping everything in its proper place. Some of these have become collector's items while others still serve to give the Irish kitchen its identity. Wooden plate racks and cutlery racks were hung from the wall, together with the old salt box and that abiding feature, the cup rack or rail – rubble or earth walls made it difficult to secure hanging hooks and the rack or rail was a natural solution. It might be a simple rectangle of painted laths or staves, or a row of pegs driven into a painted backboard, but then as now it displayed a dashing collection of cups and colanders, enamelled jugs and toasting forks, butter pats, wooden beetles for mashing potatoes and perhaps the odd horseshoe, hung open-end up for luck.

One feature, which has virtually disappeared, but might be revived, is the clevy, a pair of curved wooden hooks originally designed to carry roasting spits. The clevy could be found cut into the woodwork on the top half of a country dresser or set over the hearth with a storage shelf built into it. Designs and names varied from region to region: what was referred to as a spit rack in Tipperary was a clevy in the Comeragh mountains in County Cork. The name, imported with the early English settlers, became so much a part of the language that the clevy or *cléibhí* came to mean any place of storage beside the fire – on the Aran Islands the *cléibhí* meant a fireside hole for keeping tea and tobacco dry.

The Irish, like their Celtic cousins in Scotland, Wales and Brittany, have a strong sympathy with their recent rural past. Even if a kitchen is equipped with all the accoutrements of modern culinary practice there would is certainly likely to be some feature that any great-grandmother would look upon with affectionate recognition – small painted wooden boxes, willow-work bird cages, a baby's rush-work rattle, a decorative wicker potato skib or the holy shelf where the red votive lamp would stand, lighting the religious pictures bought from a passing traveller and hung so they tilted down on the family at prayer.

IRISH PARLOURS

The building of magnificent manors and palatial mansions would have had little influence on the small tenant farmer, the impoverished parson or the struggling craftsman during the seventeenth and eighteenth centuries, but the great number of minor houses built across rural Ireland during the early nineteenth century certainly did. In the 1790s, John Morrison, the son of an architect and builder from Midleton, County Cork, published what amounted to a book of house plans, *Useful and Ornamental Designs in Architecture*. The aspiring homeowner could select from the book a home that would both impress his neighbours and suit the size of his purse. At one end of the scale – the bottom end – was the 'Parsonage or Farmhouse', the whole to cost less than £800; at the other end, and costing almost five times as much, was the grand 'Temporary Residence For a Nobleman whose Principal Residence is in England'. But it was the basic models such as the 'Hunting Lodge' (price £1057) and the 'Country House' (an extra £43) which spread inexorably across the Irish countryside and which were adapted in scaled-down versions to house anyone from the estate manager to the tenant farmer. Apart from the provision of servants' quarters, the conventional layout of these neat, box-like buildings was not unlike a modern, four-bedroomed executive-style house on an estate: a central front door led to a hall with a staircase leading off to the first floor and the family and guest bedrooms. The servants' garrets were squeezed into the roof space or slipped in beside a cellar or basement. Leading off the hall were a series of reception rooms with fine-sounding names such as the parlour, eating-room, withdrawing room, dining-parlour, library and study. The significance of these special rooms had a profound influence on less affluent neighbours and it was not long before the parlour came to be seen as an essential element in any new home, however humble. When the single, long room of small cottages was first partitioned off, this, the seminal parlour or 'the room', was often the only part of the house which possessed a wooden boarded floor. Into it went the best bureau and bookcase, the sewing machine and the family's musical instruments, religious prints and family portraits, the glass-fronted corner cupboard where special china was displayed, but rarely used and, perhaps, a pair of press beds.

Old sepia pictures taken in these Irish parlours sometimes show families in an uncomfortable light. The stiff pose, the

No longer the polite and chilly parlour used only on special occasions, the Irish parlour has been turned into a civilized sitting room. The half-glazed dresser is filled with books while the old settle or saddle bed – the seat slides out from a bed – stands beneath a spy-hole window.

RIGHT

This apparently peaceful picture of life in an Irish drawing room belies the restrained formality of nineteenth-century life in County Galway. The room was destined to undergo some radical and welcome changes.

silent piano, the heavy drapes at the window and the chintz-covered armchairs topped with lace antimacassars give the impression of unaccustomed formality and a degree of discomfort. In this way at least the Irish style has changed beyond recognition. The old straw seat, removed from the kitchen to the parlour because of its tendency to leak straw, gave way to seductively comfortable sofas and rattan armchairs. Soft furnishings, busy bookshelves and lightweight curtains joined company with the grandfather clock, the mahogany farmhouse sideboard and the Windsor rocking chair that traditionally furnished the parlour. Even the most disapproving elder would have to admit that altering the parlour to create a living room was a change for the better.

FIREPLACES

Central-heating systems may be clean and convenient, but they could never rival the comfort of an open fire. As a source of heat and light, the hearth was the focus of daily life, and the traditional fireplace varied from the cavernous inglenook of the well-appointed farmhouse to the tiny fireplace of the small terraced house with its tiled back and cast-iron grate. Many small homes either had the most basic chimney

*O*ld fireplaces such as this solid stone surround often lie hidden behind a wall of plasterboard. After a period when they were left out in the cold, the fireplace has returned, even to the centrally-heated home.

LEFT

*S*uitably simple treatments complement the look of the living room. Floral-patterned fabrics and deep soft furnishings enhance the clean lines and natural materials of the restored cottage parlour with its the raw stone hearth, wickerwork fire basket and Windsor-style Irish chair.

arrangement formed from a wickerwork hood, clad in clay, or lacked a chimney altogether. At the other end of the social scale, Georgian architects created majestic fire surrounds and mantelpieces where, as Molly Keane would have it in her novel *Good Behaviour*, 'the wood burned up quickly and delightfully in the high, fast-draughting Georgian grates'. Made from marble, slate, wood, and in Victorian times, from cast iron, these fireplaces featured elaborate decorative effects such as scrolls, pillars and complicated carvings.

Despite the abiding appeal of the fireside, many fireplaces were hidden away behind plasterboard or a block-work wall when central-heating systems first arrived on the scene in Ireland. Yet each fireplace has a charm of its own and deserves to be restored even if, for most of the year, the fire surround simply frames an arrangement of dried flowers or a naive, hand-painted fire screen. Exposing the old hearth has to be carried out with care, for a broad chimney could conceal a pair of flues, one leading to what would have been the kitchen fire and a second to a small, brick-lined oven where the bread used to be baked. Old flues which have been dormant for decades and soon deteriorate need fireproofing with a new liner, while cast-iron grates that had been badly corroded by rust have to be replaced with a reproduction or salvaged grate.

The old-fashioned inglenook fireplace was usually constructed in a gable or end wall, at the same time as the rest of the house. It was not the most efficient design, since it burned fuel quickly and sent much of the heat straight up the chimney. One solution was the wrought-iron fireback, which radiated heat into the room, but a more efficient answer was to install a cast-iron or steel plate stove which could be closed down overnight to give a slow burn, and opened up in the evening to provide the hypnotic heat of the open fire. The wood- and peat-burning stove, together with a wickerwork peat basket and a little candlelight, all helped to recreate the country fireside scene.

COLOUR AND TEXTURE

The uncontrived elegance of the contemporary Irish living room can usually be attributed to its subtle colours and textures, its use of natural fabrics and its relaxed, country furniture. As in the past, this is a finish that has been achieved more with ingenuity and imagination than with money and high design.

Irish householders began to dispense with their homemade limewashes and distempers when reliable paints, which contained chemical pigments, became commercially available in Ireland during the nineteenth century. A century or so later, contemporary homeowners were seeking to return to these soft and subtle finishes and to bring back the translucent colours of old Ireland.

Until the turn of the twentieth century, but well into the 1950s in remote western and northern areas, limewash was the standard paint treatment. The traditional process of making limewash began with lump lime being slaked in water to produce lime putty. This was then mixed with more water, and with tallow or linseed oil to improve its waterproofing properties. Finally pigments were added to give it colour and only then were the buckets of limewash ready to be brushed over the walls, ceilings, floors and even the thatched roof of a building. Nowadays, ready-made limewashes make life a lot easier.

Slaked lime gave the limewash useful disinfectant properties, and limewash provided a sound and natural finish. Limewash allowed the walls to breathe, which was especially important on the clay-walled homes of the south and west. Moisture in these walls was able to evaporate through traditional plasters and lime renders; non-porous, oil-based paints or renders locked in these moistures, and inevitably caused moulds to form on the walls.

Lime, used for its fungicidal properties, was also added to the milk paints of the nineteenth century, which were made with buttermilk and pigments, and buttermilk paints produced a smoother, flatter finish than the limewash. But, until the relatively recent arrival of plastic-based emulsion paints, perhaps the most popular of the homemade finishes for interiors was distemper; an inside wall would need two or three coats of translucent limewash, while distemper could create a deep, textural wash of colour in a single coat. Distemper was made by adding together whiting (a chalky material), size (preferably animal glue) and water. Its tendency to leave brushmarks was one of the reasons for its decline in the past – and for its more recent revival by home restorers who liked this textured finish. Less welcome was its tendency to rub off on anything that brushed against it, a problem that could be overcome by using a good-quality size.

The country palette of distempers, limewashes and buttermilk paints ranged from luminous whites through earthy yellows, browns and pinks, and into sharp blues and cool greens. However, until the arrival of effective, artificial light, of gas lamps and electric bulbs rather than paraffin lamps and lanterns, light-reflective colours were preferred in the country household. Lustrous whites and bright lemon yellows caught the natural light from the windows and cast it back into the room. These lighter colours were sometimes used above

waist height with a warm pink or red limewash below. Later, after a particular passion for large-patterned, light-coloured wallpapers, the householder's choice of colours widened out into warm reds, oranges and yellows and calm greens, blues and violets. The different paint effects such as stencilling, colourwashing, sponging, ragging and spattering, which were perfected in the Irish homes of the past, were also brought back into the home. Eventually the Irish paint manufacturers developed a wide range of paints, which presented a rich, but sometimes confusing, palette with which to work – the Irish solution, as always, was to mix and match and to combine methods and materials in an invariably eyecatching way.

LEFT

Warm damask drapes, Indian chintz and local rush work took the chill out of the Irish parlour. Soft colourwashes and floral prints, which echoed the summer-flowering garden, all helped to achieve the relaxed elegance of country style.

*A natural alliance of the old and the not so old, of bare stone walls and
carved wooden furniture, contributes to the look of the Irish country style, a look which
sometimes involves revealing features that have been hidden from view.*

106

FABRIC AND FURNITURE

Before the Industrial Revolution the basic materials for seat cushions, curtains and carpets were drawn from the surrounding countryside, from the blue-flowered flax that went into the local linen to the goose down and feathers that were used to fill the cushions. Country interiors, then and now, were characterized by the use of natural fabrics and materials such as linen and lace, cotton and canvas, muslin and wool. The parlour was intended to be the best-looking room in the house and efforts were constantly being made to procure new materials and eyecatching finishes. The velvets and silk damasks of the grander houses were mimicked in the small houses with cottons with block-printed designs and pretty pastoral scenes, which bore little resemblance to the country lives of the women who bought them. The highly stylized floral chintzes that had originated in India (the name was derived from the Hindu *chints* meaning painted or printed fabric) were extremely popular. And, as the Victorian factories started to mass produce their strong, rich-patterned cloths, their heavy drapes and tasselled tiebacks, the fabrics were promptly adopted for the Irish parlour, which descended into the gloom of that era.

Eventually natural finishes such as coir carpeting, jute rugs, sea-grass baskets and linen throws, accompanied by a casual blend of architectural features and furniture, came to the rescue of the parlour. There was a time when the meagre, but precious free-standing furniture in most modest country homes could have fitted on to the back of a hand cart. Some furniture was integral to the house: the built-in seats by a Sligo hearth; fireside wall cupboards formed from recesses in the walls; the great press that separated the kitchen and parlour in some western farmhouse; or the plain fireside salt hole built into almost every country cabin wall. In the sensitively restored home, features like these, which form an important piece of Ireland's country past, have been preserved wherever possible. Rather than emphasizing a particular period or theme, the living room tended towards a relaxed alliance of old country pieces and good contemporary craft work. Traditional, wooden furniture such as the sideboard and the Windsor rocking chair, and sofas and armchairs chosen for comfort rather than fashionable conformity, found a place here. It was a casual arrangement that sometimes ran the risk of achieving the effect, described by Molly Keane in *Full House*, where the occupant of the room 'moved among this deplorable confusion with entire ease and comfort, found what he wanted when he wanted it and where he expected to find it, and never showed any signs of distress at the discomfort with which he was surrounded'.

In one living room, a dado rail might divide melon-yellow walls that served as a backcloth to a deeply cushioned chintz-covered sofa, an old Irish, black mahogany chest and a contemporary trestle table, stood on a floor of lightly limed, salvaged pine floorboards. In another setting, a green enamel box stove might stand, blazing with heat, beneath an age-old oak mantelpiece, surrounded by a collection of crisp, green cane chairs, and with a fiercely modern rag rug at its feet. These are rooms where there is no necessity for slavishly following convention, where a wicker bicycle basket serves as a magazine store, CDs stand stacked in a converted herb rack and a collections of methers (traditional Irish drinking vessels) are displayed in a glass-fronted medicine cabinet.

One of the key elements, both here and in the rest of the house, has been the use of recycled materials. Now better organized than it ever was, the architectural salvage industry in Ireland has become a constant source of useful ideas and materials, although, from reclaimed floorboards to damaged but repairable furniture, salvaged materials were nothing new to country people who usually had the space as well as the inclination to collect and store 'just in case'.

A look at the traditional Irish parlour and kitchen reveals that these rooms were created by people with a deep understanding of natural materials, a sympathetic sense of design and an instinctive approach to making the most of not very much.

Since those days, Irish homes have changed dramatically: heat and light at the touch of a switch; space-age fabrics and hard-wearing, washable materials; high-tech kitchens, washing machines, computers, telephones and all those other time-saving gadgets that a century ago, would have seemed inconceivable. Yet, despite the temptations of a push-button, throw-away lifestyle, most contemporary householders still prefer to live in warm and welcoming surroundings with which their predecessors would have every sympathy.

'Beauty is all very well at first sight;
but who ever looks at it when it has been in the
house three days?'

G. B. SHAW

Irish Bedrooms and Bathrooms

OPPOSITE PAGE
*Bedrooms and bathrooms are relative
newcomers to Ireland's small country homes.
But, from a quaint collection of old medicine
containers, above, to the traditional method
of making steps to the bedroom, opposite, the
Irish demonstrate a flair for the unexpected.*

WINDOWS CURTAINED WITH DELICATE IRISH LACE, brass bed-
steads made with best Irish linen and covered with traditional handmade quilts, painted blanket chests and rush-seated rocking chairs –
nowhere did the scene change so radically as upstairs in the Irish country home,
where crowded rooms and cluttered attics gave way to spacious bedrooms, sublime
bathrooms and lively studios and workrooms.

Country bedrooms, characterized by their natural simplicity, sensible storage and
attractive beds, have altered since the days when they were filled with the family
beds and stores of fruit and vegetables. Bathrooms were never there in the beginning, but, having found their proper place in the home, they have tended to contain
all the traditional elements of Irish country style from the painted, wooden wall cabinets to the wickerwork laundry basket.

STAIRCASE

The staircase, the most complicated piece of joinery in any house, was a relative
newcomer to the small Irish country home. In western Ireland especially, the longhouse tradition gave homes a linear layout, where the pig, poultry and house cow

occupied the lower part of the house while the family worked, ate and slept in the upper part. A loft ladder of rough-hewn saplings was all that was needed to reach the little attics, tucked in under the pitched thatch roof, where the harvest of fruit, vegetables and animal fodder was stored. Eventually the animals were moved to their own byre away from the house and the family took over the whole building. Bare walls were plastered and limewashed, a fresh floor of pebbles or pounded clay was laid down and, occasionally, a new fireplace was constructed against the end wall. The house would be divided perhaps by a wattle and daub partition, but a ladder rather than a staircase would still serve the attic space. Eventually these two- or four-roomed longhouses grew upwards into thatched mansions, as they were sometimes known, with a row of low dormer windows tucked in under the eaves to light the upper rooms. Country people seemed reluctant to break with tradition and increase their floor space by building on to the back of the house – the two-storey farmhouse that is no more than one room deep is still common across the country. A house that is only as wide as its downstairs rooms has little space for, in Molly Keane's words, a 'romantic staircase perpetually pleasing,' and in older Irish homes they can descend at an alarm-

ABOVE

Where space is at a premium, a half turn added to a flight of stairs avoids creating a dangerously steep descent.

RIGHT

A central staircase descends into a wood-panelled hall filled with an eclectic collection of memorabilia.

ing rate from a landing bedroom into kitchens and halls, or else curl round the gable-end hearth in a precipitous ascent. (In 1866 the Royal Agricultural Society of Ireland recorded its gratitude to one landowner for building his farm cottages with 'a very convenient form of step ladder or cheap stair ... which gives sufficient width for the foot to allow the ladder to be sheeted at the back'.)

One contemporary answer to the perils of a steep and narrow staircase was to reconstruct a dog-leg or half-turn flight against a gable wall. Another sensible solution was to double the width of the central corridor which leads through from the front door

to the back in so many small country homes. This generally created enough space for a flight of stairs to a small hall above. The business of building homes with a central passage between the front and the back of the house had its particular advantages, as J. M. Synge noted during his long stay on the Aran Islands: 'Nearly all the cottages are built, like this one, with two doors opposite each other, the more sheltered of which lies open all day to give light to the interior.' But if the wind was in the wrong direction, the islanders, few of whom could afford a clock in the early twentieth century, quickly lost track of time. 'If the wind is northerly the south door is opened, and the shadow of the door-post moving across the kitchen indicates the hour; as soon, however, as the wind changes to the south the other door is opened, and the people, who never think of putting up a primitive dial, are at a loss.'

Stairs, when they were added to cottages such as these, might be boxed in with painted deal panels or the flight left open – a better arrangement as far as younger members of the family were concerned, since they could use them as ringside seats when their kitchen became the focus of an impromptu neighbourhood party. The staircase, then and now, was often the first architectural feature a visitor encountered. A stair carpet would have been a rare luxury for most people. Instead the bare boards might be grained to give a passable imitation of mahogany or treated to a light paint finish, which not only brightened the look of the steps but helped the householder find his or her way to bed by the light of the lantern. In the contemporary home, the lighting, layout and look of the stairs were dictated by safety considerations: ill-lit stairs, highly polished steps or the potentially dangerous combination of young children and a steep, spiral staircase were best avoided. Nevertheless, the look of the Irish stairway was rarely restrained. Given that the highest uninterrupted wall in the house usually occupied the stairwell, this was the ideal place for a full-length, faded tapestry or a portrait collection of someone else's ancestors. Period details, such as moulded handrails, finely carved newel posts or barley-twist balustrades, and decorative effects ranging from a subtle colourwash (light colours were preferable on a poorly lit stairwell) to a bold stencilled border at dado-rail height all contributed to a distinctive staircase.

BEDROOMS

In the single-storey longhouse, as in the modern bungalow, the sleeping quarters led off from the hall. The single bedroom of the smaller cottage looked like a dormitory, with the family beds, curtained off for privacy with printed fabrics, lining the walls of the little room. One bed, however, that never left the kitchen was the outshot bed or hag, as it was sometimes known. The outshot, a comparatively common feature in those country homes that lay north and west of an imaginary line between County Galway and County Antrim, was more of an alcove than a bedroom. While it has long disappeared from most renovated country kitchens, the old outshot may still be present, hidden behind a pair of cupboard doors in the unreconstructed farmhouse. The alcove, scarcely bigger than the double bed that fitted inside, was built into the back wall of the house, comfortably close to the hearth. Insulated with its own ceiling of woven grass or rush matting (and later with wallpaper or out-of-date newspapers pasted to the ceiling and hidden under a coat of whitewash) it might sleep the working heads of the household, who were last to bed and first to rise, or the ageing grandparent whose old bones benefited from the constant heat of the hearth. Another cosy kitchen bed was the box bed, built into one corner of the room and sometimes concealed behind deal board partitions. Box beds saved heat and space: woollen curtains, hung from a rail attached to the side of the bed, could be drawn at night to keep in the heat and a bunk bed for the children was often placed above the bed. Especially popular in Ulster, the box beds were probably introduced by Scottish settlers who traditionally enjoyed the comfort of sleeping by the glowing embers of the fire. In parts of southern Ireland country families managed quite happily without any fixed bed, using instead the forerunner of the modern futon, a thick-plaited straw mattresses, which would be laid out on the floor at night and rolled up out of the way during the day.

Beds needed high, cot-like sides to accommodate the layers of mattresses on which the sleeper lay. Tough, elastic cords made from hemp rope, or preferably from plaits of fir-tree branches retrieved from the peat bog, were strung across between the headboard and footboard to form the base of the

Taken for granted for too long, the simple charms of Irish style are returning to favour. This was the austere bachelor's bedroom of Dublin-born playwright George Bernard Shaw.

bed. These could carry the weight of two mattresses, the first made of plaited straw and the second from hessian feed sacks sewn together and filled with fresh, loose straw at threshing time. The farmer who kept a gaggle of geese would save the soft down of the goose feathers after his birds had been plucked for market and, when he had sufficient, use it to fill feather mattresses and pillows. Goose-down bedding was regarded as a luxury (poorer people had to be content with bog cotton as a pillow filler) and goose-down mattresses were frequently mentioned in old wills and inventories. When a bride moved to her new home, she would be expected to take her feather mattress as part of her dowry. She often took her bed as well, provided it could be moved. Many Irish beds were part of the

*Together with the iron bedstead covered with its cottage quilt,
the washstand and bowl, the pitcher of water and the chamber pot were
a feature of life before bathrooms.*

*An Irish country bedroom is faithfully recreated at the
Bunratty Folk Park in County Clare. Places like these, which have
saved so many of Ireland's historic, humble houses, are a rich resource
and a treasure house of ideas.*

fixtures and fittings and as indispensable to the house as its doors or windows. The outshot bed was an integral part of the fireside walls, while the cosy canopy or camp bed, a pine-built bed with a rush mattress, curtained sides and an arched, canopy-like roof, was built into the bedroom.

Another favourite piece of bedroom furniture, the traditional four-poster bed, draped against the draughts with white work such as muslin, still makes a special contribution to the charm and comfort of the contemporary Irish bedroom, although low cottage ceilings where one could, as Yeats put it, 'listen to the brawling of a sparrow in the eaves' sometimes call for a compromise on size. The Irish ancestor of the four-poster was the tester bed, a modest copy of the grand country-house bed and often adapted by those whose purse did not run to drapes or cloth to take woven hangings of straw which curtained off the sleeping quarters. When the ceiling of the tester bed was boarded over, it provided a useful storage solution, as a place to put hat boxes or the rabbit gun, and even, in the humblest of homes, as a safe place for the household hens to roost.

Irish emigrants took the idea of the space-saving outshot or bed annexe with them to Australia and America, along with that other Irish bed, equally economic with space, the press bed. A press was, and still is in rural Ireland, the name for a cupboard or wardrobe and a press bed was literally a bed in a cupboard. At night the press bed was folded down, but by day it was artfully hidden behind its cupboard doors. Equally suited to the small country home was the truckle bed, a low divan that slid beneath the master bed during the day. Nevertheless, the truckle, press bed and tester were all falling out of favour by the late nineteenth century, when that most enduring of all bed designs, the iron or brass bedstead started to slip into Irish country homes. Those who regarded the old-style wooden bed and its straw mattress as a harbinger of disease actively encouraged its arrival. In fact the straw mattresses (and the skills which went into its making) survived well into the twentieth century not least because the solid straw mattress served to protect the valuable feather mattress from the ravages of the iron bedsprings beneath.

ABOVE

A luxurious four poster, left, and a snug single bed with a whimsical, shell-decorated headboard provide two examples of Irish bedroom furniture.

ABOVE

A wardrobe built from recycled wood makes the most of the limited space in a small country bedroom where storage is scarce.

After a spell in the outhouse and even in the fields, where the old bedhead might usefully plug a gap in the hedge, the metal bedstead has been rescued, recycled and restored to the bedroom, along with the traditional baby's bed, the cradle. Wooden or wicker cradles were once made by the thousand in Ireland and were often kept in the kitchen, where the infant could be rocked to sleep while his or her mother worked at her spinning wheel. At one end of the social scale, the family would commission the master basket maker to construct the traditional Moses basket-cradle with its wickerwork tray and supporting legs; at the other it was simply fashioned from a few planks, painted and lined with straw. J. M. Synge described one made 'with rough wood fastened underneath to serve as rockers, and all the time I am in my room I can hear it bumping on the floor with extraordinary violence'.

The rocking cradle tradition survived and the creaking Moses

basket made a sensible contribution to the small cottage bedrooms with ceilings that sweep down almost to the skirting boards. Modestly lit by floor-level dormer windows, small rooms such as these need careful treatment to avoid becoming too busy and overcrowded. Tester beds hung with a lace-edged valance instead of the traditional full-length drapes, lightweight duvets on dark pine beds covered by day with a traditional patchwork quilt, and restored iron beds, rejuvenated with a new mattress, all contribute to the good looks of country bedrooms. Blanket or clothes chests at the end of the bed, dowry chests – a blanket chest built on top of a simple chest of drawers – and a sturdy Irish country chair also find floor space in the contemporary bedroom.

The one problem in all these small, country bedrooms is storage. Large wardrobes rarely fit beneath a sloping ceiling and are better employed as a storage solution in a hall or beneath an open staircase. One solution is to use built-in storage cupboards and, rather than closing them with conventional store-bought doors, using oiled pine or painted board doors made from recycled wood and pierced perhaps with a shamrock or diamond design.

Bedrooms tend to acquire pieces of furniture that have fallen out of favour elsewhere in the house. In Georgian times it might have been a rugged old walnut bureau, replaced in the drawing room by a more fashionable mahogany piece. In modern times it is more likely to be a pine corner cupboard or a pair of cane chairs, relegated to the bedroom because they no longer conform to the look of the kitchen. These old pieces are always preferable to standard, purpose-made bedroom furniture, especially when they have been treated with a striking paint effect such as being covered in two contrasting coats of matt emulsion that are then roughly rubbed down to reveal the different strata of paint. Another popular treatment is to lime the woodwork by painting a coat of white latex paint on to the stripped-down wood and wiping it down before the paint dries.

The washstand with its jug and basin was a familiar sight in Ireland's Victorian bedrooms. The better washstands had a hole cut in the top, to take a patterned bowl, and a splash-board, sometimes tiled, set around three sides of the top. After a spell when they were left out in the cold, the washstands

LEFT
Since it had to be filled by hand, the old hip bath has become no more than a curious conversation piece.

BELOW
A first-floor bedroom has been converted into a relaxed bathing place complete with its free-standing enamelled bath, old-fashioned brass taps and a wickerwork laundry basket.

OPPOSITE PAGE
Bathing in splendour, the graceful glories of the Georgian era make a classic case for spending time in the bathroom.

were brought back to the bedroom, often adapted to hold a small hand basin.

With the introduction of modern central heating, there is no longer a need for the open fire in the bedroom, but the neat little wrought-iron grates of the old farmhouse still make an attractive contribution to any country bedroom and the perfect place for a handmade wicker basket filled with an autumn collection of pine-scented fir cones.

BATHROOMS

Although the bathroom was the youngest room in most Irish country homes, it was a recent addition that quickly came under the Irish influence. As with the rest of the home, it is often the idiosyncratic touches that contribute to a sense of Irish style: a briar basket filled with dried rose leaves beside a claw-footed bath, a collection of Victorian shaving mugs in an elegant, glass-fronted cabinet or a painted pie chest decorated with a shamrock-shaped hole or Cupid's bow trim.

When old Irish homes change hands the bathroom is frequently the first room to be targeted for renovation, not least

and sinks set in marble, or glazed tiles that blaze with warm oranges and yellows and walls finished in ochre earth colours all conjure up the sensations of the southern climate. Substituting an open shower for a bath, where the walls and floors are tiled and the water drains out under the floor, save space in the small bathroom and add a touch of Tuscan warmth to the room. The antiquated glories of the Georgian era is another favourite theme, where an eclectic mix of fixtures and fittings, of a roll-top, enamelled bath encased in a mahogany surround, for example, or a pedestal-style sink mounted on an ancient, cast-iron sewing machine stand, bring to mind the old days when nothing seemed to be new. Handsome if heavy pieces of furniture could add to the effect – a tired, but sturdy chaise-longue, a large linen chest or a towel rail made from a kitchen clothes horse. A warming finishing touch is to have a small peat fire burning in one of the little, cast-iron fireplaces sometimes found in old country bathrooms.

With over 2000 miles of coastline around Ireland, seashore themes also have an abiding appeal. Wall finishes range from a seashell pink to a marine-like bluey green; sinks and baths are set in salt-washed planks; natural floor finishes such as coir and seagrass are preferred to the old, chilly linoleum; and decorative details such as shell and pebble collections, or a vase full of dried foreshore flowers, give the rooms their finishing touch.

Willow, rush and *súgán* or straw, traditional materials of the Irish countryside, also have a special place in the bathroom. A willow-work potato pannier, adapted to serve as a laundry basket, or a handmade mat of bulrushes from the rush makers of the Slievebourne Co-operative in Strokestown, County Roscommon, provide a welcome, natural touch. Since straw was kinder to an animal than raw leather, *súgán* or straw work was traditionally used as a harness for young horses being broken in, but *súgán* was also plaited into screens, mats, mattresses and baskets, and a *súgán* of fresh oat straw adds a mellow feel to the bathroom.

Since there are still plenty of period Irish homes equipped with nothing more than a single cold-water tap, cottage bathrooms often need to be designed from scratch, giving new homeowners the opportunity to let their imaginations run wild.

because so many Irish bathrooms were added as an afterthought to some cramped and chilly corner of the house. Until the end of the nineteenth century, and well beyond in remote rural areas, the tin bath, the chamber pot and the outdoor earth closet or privy met most people's needs. When the privy finally was pulled down and the old hip bath hung up, the bathroom might be slipped in at the back beside the dairy, traditionally built on the cool, north side of the house, or set in a purpose-built annexe close to the kitchen. These early bathroom builders had yet to experience the pleasures of a relaxing soak in the tub while watching the sunset framed in the cottage window.

The bathroom might be the youngest room in the house, but period-style fittings on original, or reproduction, fixtures help to achieve a country feel and suggest the style that never was. Plain white paint finishes are complemented by simple fabrics – cotton or muslin curtains hung at the window from a painted wooden pole or the shelves beneath a basin hidden behind a piece of embroidered muslin.

Sometimes the Mediterranean-like finishes of the south-west are brought into the bathroom. Old-fashioned brass taps

'Do not pay much attention to labelling; if a plant is not worth knowing it is not worth growing'

Irish Gardens

Wreaths of Virginia creeper, above, surround a cottage window in County Cork while a rock pool in County Down, opposite, is shadowed by a late spring show of rhododendron and azalea. Home to some internationally famous gardens, Ireland is also renowned for its cottage gardens and private demesnes.

IRELAND HAS GAINED A REPUTATION for being a gardener's paradise. Home to some historic and outstanding gardens, Ireland is firmly established on the international garden tour circuit, which draws visitors from around the world. But this island's genteel climate and warming gulf stream waters have not only produced some of the best-known gardens in Europe, but also nurtured some highly influential gardeners, including William Robinson. This was the Irish gardener who has been called the 'father of the English garden' and who brought about a horticultural revolution when he and his friend, the eminent English garden designer Gertrude Jekyll, advocated a more informal approach to garden design. Robinson's inspiration came, not from the magnificent manicured acres of Ireland's great and grand gardens but from the charming informality of the cottage-style garden that is still so much a feature of Ireland today, and it is this fertile patchwork of small country gardens that really brings colour to the Emerald Isle.

THE IRISH EDEN

The 20-hectare (50-acre) gardens of Powerscourt at the foot of the Great Sugar Loaf Mountain near Dublin rank among Ireland's horticultural aristocracy. With their sweeping terraces, ornamental lakes, rambling walks and secret hollows, these grand gardens were originally laid out in the mid-eighteenth century. The eccentric

ABOVE

In the secret corner of an Irish garden, a cascading water feature creates the high humidity conditions which these moisture-loving ferns require.

LEFT

Dramatic rock formations frame the entrance to the Grotto at Powerscourt Gardens in the foothills of the Wicklow mountains. The Grotto was built during the eighteenth century from petrified sphagnum found on the banks of the River Dargle.

with subtropical flora, New Zealand ferns and a rare collection of Bonsai trees, Ilnacullin with its Grecian temple and neo-classical follies possesses all the formal finery of a grand garden. There is another Garinish Island around the coast in Kenmare Bay, County Kerry, which supports a thriving community of Australian tree ferns (*Dicksonia antarctica*), euphorbia and other foreign imports including the Australasian callistemon or bottlebrush. Like so many other Irish gardens, this island, originally planted in the mid-nineteenth century, benefits from the warming currents of the gulf stream.

At Glenveagh in County Donegal, a Gothic castle broods on the banks of Lough Veagh. Here a succession of American owners from the 1870s to the 1980s worked the thin soils until they could support a collection of rare and tender shrubs, together with a woodland glade of rhododendrons threaded with paths which blaze with azalea blossom every spring. Rhododendrons and azaleas also thrive on the light acid soils of the drumlin-dotted Rowallane in County Down, a garden designed by the distinguished plantsman Hugh Armytage Moore in the early years of the twentieth century in the style of William Robinson.

Robinson died in 1935, but his writings have continued to persuade succeeding generations of gardeners to adopt his more informal approach to garden design, replacing their borders of tender bedding plants with a subtle mixture of native and exotic plants and underplanting their grass swards with swathes of flowering bulbs. Born in County Down in 1838, William Robinson started his gardening career as a humble water carrier at Curraghmore gardens in County Waterford. By 1870 he had become the most widely read gardening author and was well on the way to changing the whole face of gardening.

The young William had been compelled to earn a wage early on in life. His father had deserted the family, eloping with the wife of his employer and setting sail with her for America. William took the job at Curraghmore to help his family. However, after an argument with the head gardener, he opened all the greenhouses in his care on one of the coldest nights of the year and then abandoned them, setting off on foot for Dublin, where he was to become an apprenticed gardener at the National Botanic Garden. By the time he was twenty-six he

architect Daniel Robertson, who is said to have been carried around the estate in a wheelbarrow in an inspired but inebriated condition, redesigned the gardens in the nineteenth century. Mount Stewart near Belfast in County Down, its neat acres quartered into thematic rooms such as the Spanish, Italian and Shamrock gardens, is another of Ireland's great gardens.

Then there are the forgotten ghosts of gardens, such as a walled garden at Castletown Cox in County Kilkenny where, at the turn of the twentieth century, Lady Eva Wyndham-Quin meticulously maintained her white garden with its matching menagerie of white peacocks, white hens, white dogs and white goats. There are island gardens such as Ilnacullin or Garinish Island, transformed from a bare, rocky island into an exotic fantasy by the English architect Harold Peto in 1910. Surrounded by the waters of Bantry Bay in County Cork and filled

A bed of purple candelabra primula *peppers a lakeside in the gardens of Mount Stewart House in County Down. Introduced in the 1920s, the plants thrive in the Mount Stewart microclimate.*

Celebrating the fact that Ireland is the only country in the world with a musical instrument as its national emblem, this topiary harp grows in the Shamrock Garden at Mount Stewart.

had moved to England and been appointed a foreman at the Royal Botanic Society's Garden in Regent's Park, London. From here on his rise in the ranks of the gardening world was meteoric, culminating in 1870 when he completed writing *The English Flower Garden*, a garden book that would outsell all others. The Robinsonian approach influenced the wild informality of Mount Usher gardens in County Wicklow, originally laid out along the banks of the meandering River Varty by a nineteenth-century Dubliner, Edward Walpole. To the south in County Cork the banks of the Awbeg River provided another Robinsonian setting for a collection of magnolias, hoherias and rare trees at Annes Grove.

A plant-filled urn sits in stately splendour above a garden bench overhung with the scent of roses. Mount Stewart, which ranks among the most beautiful gardens in Ireland, has helped to put the country on the international garden tour circuit.

A small host of gardeners was required to manage these nineteenth-century labour-intensive estates and the rising labour costs of the twentieth century saw a dramatic decrease in their numbers and a corresponding rise in the do-it-yourself, owner-gardens. One Irish example is the country classic Butterstream in County Mayo, created from a heavy clay frost pocket of farmland by its owner Jim Reynolds, armed with little more than a spade, a shovel and a saw. Another is the full-flowering urban oasis of the Dillon garden in Dublin, a clever creation of little gardens arranged around a central lawn.

Other, older gardens have been brought back to life by an Irish government restoration programme, benefiting places like Birr Castle in County Offaly where what was once the world's largest reflecting telescope towers over a collection of more than a thousand flowering shrubs and trees. More recent beneficiaries of the programme have been the Creagh gardens in County Cork, their good looks inspired by a painting by the French artist Rousseau; the *ferme ornée* Larchill Arcadian gardens in County Kildare with its Gothic follies and Classical gazebos; and Ardgillan Castle gardens in County Dublin with a Victorian glasshouse, vegetable potager and a woodland walk that is yet another testimony to the great William Robinson.

Many of these plant-rich paradises are open to the public. Some of the gardens such as Glenveagh Castle and Ilnacullin have passed into state ownership; others such as Mount Stewart and Rowallane are managed by the National Trust and these public pleasure grounds, which attract visitors worldwide, have formed the foundation for Ireland's reputation as a Garden of Eden.

However, it is the private plots and secret demesnes of the enthusiastic amateur that underpin the real flowering of Ireland. Until the middle of the twentieth century, the owners who collected their prize rosettes at the local horticultural show mostly owed their success to their faithful retainers, the gardeners whose own five-to-nine-o'clock shift kept the Irish cottage garden in good heart. At work in the gardens of the grand house, the gardeners devoted their energies to raising the thousands of bedding plants required to produce the swathes of colour their employers so admired. The suppliers who benefited from the sales of their aster, stock, phlox, primula and antirrhinum seeds supported the practice: 'Those who rail against summer bedding make a fanciful entity called Fashion responsible for what they deem a low-toned folly,' wrote one Victorian seedsman. 'But we may conclude, without violence to reason, that the prevalence of summer bedding indicates its usefulness as a sort of visible antidote to the gloom we are so often involved in by our peculiar climate.'

From the countryman's point of view, the massed colours were neither useful nor edible and, at home in their own cottage-sized plots and allotments, the gardener and his neighbours grew a dense concentration of fruit, flowers, vegetables and herbs. To the casual observer, these pocket-sized gardens seemed disordered and chaotic places; but to the experienced eye, they were well-organized and intensely productive gardens. Pinks and pansies edged a path to the back door; the Dutch hoe kept the self-seeding hollyhocks at bay from a row of broad beans or a clump of runner beans trained up a wigwam of hazel canes; lavender and rosemary grew up through a ground cover of forget-me-nots; a pair of fruit trees, entangled with honeysuckle, framed ordered rows of leeks and onions. Husband and wife traditionally divided their responsibilities, she looking after the herbs and flowers, he growing the fruit and vegetables, while the whole family helped out at harvest time. Families with a little more growing space at their dis-

posal would keep the flowers and herbs close to the house and plant their parsnips, peas and potatoes in neat rows that ran down to the hen run and pig pen at the bottom of the garden. Beyond, there might be an herb-rich orchard, regularly grazed or scythed for a little winter's hay. Growing their honeysuckle around the porch and their roses around the gate, the cottager and his wife would take stock of their garden on a summer's

Ireland's reputation as a gardener's paradise has been enhanced by owner-gardeners and enthusiasts like Jim Reynolds who created the imaginative Butterstream in County Mayo.

The casual informality of the Robinsonian style, seen here at Mount Usher Gardens in County Wicklow, was inspired by one of Ireland's most famous gardeners, William Robinson.

A strong sense of design and colour can create a horticultural oasis in town or country. Here in the Dillon's Garden, Dublin, box hedging and topiary stand beside a stone sphinx.

TOP

A hornbeam allée at Birr Castle demesne in County Offaly focuses on a distant statue. Techniques like these were scaled down and adapted by the cottage gardener.

Romantic seclusion has been a feature of Irish gardens ever since Dublin's Mary Delany and the satirist Jonathan Swift created their own romantic gardens in the eighteenth century. This tranquil garden is at Creagh Gardens near Skibbereen in County Cork.

evening, admiring the sight and scent of their flowering plants and the darkening shapes and shadows of their fruit bushes and vegetables. They would never have guessed that, one day, their horticultural methods would become the celebrated and captivating cottage-style garden.

Now a new generation of owner-gardeners have become custodians of this rural patchwork of private gardens, managing anything from a pint-sized backyard to a rambling country demesne, and brightening the country from fertile County Down to fruitful County Cork. Quietly pleased and invariably modest about their achievements, Ireland's weekend gardeners have continued to make the most of this productive place.

COUNTRY ORIGINS

The prehistory of the Irish garden lies in a long-lost past. Ireland has fewer native plants and animals than neighbouring Britain since, as the glaciers of the last Ice Age retreated, fewer species managed to make the journey west before the land corridors to Europe finally slipped beneath the sea. As a consequence Ireland has no indigenous mole, weasel, wild cat or snake and its natural stock of flowering plants and ferns is just over half that found on the neighbouring mainland. Yet Ireland shelters some unique plants in some remarkable environments: the solid colonies of sea asters and sea lavender on the salt marshes of Strangford Lough, County Down; the electric-blue spring gentian hidden away in the limestone crevices of the Burren; the rare pink-flowered St Dabeoc's heather on the native heaths of County Mayo and Galway; and the blue large-flowered butterwort or bog violet of west Cork and Kerry. As the hand of man imported and added new species to this natural fauna Ireland has become a collecting bowl of curiosities where palm trees thrive under the spring rains of County Kerry and the scarlet-flowered rhododendron grows with the tenacious vigour of a weed.

Ireland had already gained a reputation for fruitful productivity 1300 years ago. The eighth-century scholar Bede noted Ireland's profusion of vines and plentiful supplies of milk and honey. 'Ireland is far more favoured than Britain by latitude, and by its mild and healthy climate,' he wrote, adding that in this hospitable place 'there is no need to store hay in winter.'

Irish gardens, Irish plants: Ireland has become a collecting bowl for wild and cultivated flora from sea lavender (Limonium vulgare), *below,* butterwort *(pinquicola grandiflora), below left, spring gentian* (Gentiana verna), *below right and rhododendron, bottom.*

Early designs provided protection for the plantsman's crops. The knot garden, introduced by the Normans, is seen here at Castletown Cox in County Kilkenny.

In the early days, some of the plants imported from overseas were so precious that they were kept under lock and key in the walled garden.

Up until the seventeenth century the Irish gardeners cultivated their crops of caraway, fennel, feverfew, hollyhocks, roses and southernwood. Occasionally they protected their plantings with clipped box hedges arranged in the knot designs that had been introduced by the Norman settlers, but their choice of plants was limited to those drawn from European stocks. All that was to change when, in the seventeenth century, exotic new fruits, flowers and vegetables began to reach Ireland, especially from the New World. After the introduction, reputedly by Sir Walter Raleigh, of the tobacco plant from Virginia and the potato from South America, there was a botanical scramble to collect new and exciting plants from across the globe. In the 1690s Sir Arthur and Lady Helen Rawdon of Moira, County Down, sent their gardener all the way to the West Indies to fill twenty cases with tropical plants that would furnish their new (and Ireland's first) heated conservatory at Moira. Gradually the trickle of new plants turned into a torrent. Pelargoniums arrived from southern Africa, chrysanthemums, peonies and roses from China and dahlias from Latin America. Rare exotics like fuschias and rhododendrons turned out to be so suited to the Irish climate that they soon seeded themselves outside the garden and colonized the surrounding countryside. (It seems that the imported rhododendron was only recolonizing its old territory: according to recent pollen analysis, rhododendrons grew in Ireland up until the last Ice Age.) Meanwhile technical advances in glass and cast-iron technology and the consequent spread of the greenhouse and heated conservatory led to the widespread cultivation of exotics like peaches, palms and citrus trees.

Establishing collections of these new, foreign imports was the preserve of the affluent landowner; but their care, cultivation and, most importantly, propagation lay in the hands of the country gardeners, who were not slow to introduce the new plants into their own and their neighbours' cottage gardens. And while the great gardens followed the fashionable designs of the day, the smaller gardens followed in their footsteps.

The troubled state of Irish politics had meant that, apart from places like Carrickfergus Castle in County Antrim, Lis-

more Castle in County Waterford and the Earl of Cork's estate at Youghal, Ireland had inherited few of the great Elizabethan and Jacobean gardens. Nevertheless the grand styles of the seventeenth century, with their terraces, gravel walks, parterres, walled gardens and artful water features were common enough, even if relatively few survive today. In the latter part of the seventeenth century, when French and Dutch Huguenots lost the freedom to worship in their own countries, those who moved to Ulster brought with them not only their linen-making skills, but their own seeds, seedlings and horticultural expertise. Irish Protestants, in deference to their Dutch counterparts, often adopted the neat and ordered elements of Dutch garden design and followed with enthusiasm the new ideas on raising fruit and vegetables.

By the eighteenth century, large gardens such as those at Kilruddery House, owned by the earls of Meath and set in the

RIGHT

The flood of new plants brought back from abroad turned into a torrent during the seventeenth and eighteenth centuries. These exotic imports were quick to spread to the cottage gardens as working gardeners brought their cuttings home.

As the design of Irish gardens came under the influence of Dutch, English and French designs, such as the one recreated here in County Cork, one admiring eighteenth-century gardener remarked: 'Nature has been profusely beneficent to Ireland.'

foothills of the Wicklow Mountains, were following the school of Le Nôtre, that influential family of French gardeners responsible for so much Gallic formality. With its pair of canals, its ponds, parterres and mathematically precise paths, Kilruddery remains one of the best-preserved French-style gardens in Ireland. Later in the eighteenth century, Irish garden styles took a more relaxed turn when the Dublin dean and satirist Jonathan Swift began to till the soil of Naboth's Vineyard, as he called his plot of ground near St Patrick's Cathedral in Dublin. A keen fruit-tree grower, Jonathan Swift and his gardener friend Mary Delany, wife of the Dean of Down, inspired a less formal, more romantic style of gardening with their designs for places such as Caledon in County Kerry with its bizarre folly built from cattle knuckle bones and Mary's own 4.5-hectare (11-acre) demesne at Delville in the Dublin suburbs. By Mary's own account Delville was 'a wilderness of sweets' with its rustic seats and shell grotto, its temple and orangery. She and her husband had to protect their plantings from a predatory resident herd of red deer but still managed to establish a poetic garden full of jasmine, gillyflowers, perfumed roses, primroses and sweet briars. To add a further touch of romanticism to the place, they even employed an Irish harpist to play occasionally under an arbour of nut trees.

Mary Delany did not live long enough to see the establishment of Dublin's National Botanic Gardens near to Delville in 1795; nor did she have to witness the effects of the Great Famine on Irish gardens great and small. Famine-relief projects, designed to give work to country people in desperate circumstances, added miles of new walls and strange follies to the nineteenth-century demesnes, but emigration and the resulting rural depopulation saw many thousands of small gardens simply slip back into the wilderness.

One Irish gardener who devoted herself to famine relief in County Longford was the nineteenth-century novelist Maria Edgeworth, author of *Castle Rackrent* and so well known that she once received a famine-relief parcel from the United States addressed simply to 'Miss Maria, Ireland'. Maria Edgeworth was a great exponent of the Irish owner-gardener, cultivating her roses and lilies and indulging her passion for 'a gay or even a shabby garden – it is a rest to the mind and at all times a relief'.

The country people around her, who had mostly been managing their plots of ground out of economic necessity and who, as one old Galway gardener put it, were totally 'self efficient', demonstrated their customary ingenuity in keeping fertility high and costs low. Cartloads of seaweed were used to dress thin soils; homemade versions of stock-proof wire were made from thorns bound into lengths of *súgán*; barrels of animal blood from the local abattoir were administered to the onion patch until the soil turned blue-black; and a potent, if pungent, liquid fertilizer was made by steeping sheep droppings and wool in buckets of water. When the old cart tracks were metalled and taken over by the resident mileman or road cleaner, his sweepings of grit, leafmould and soil were used to make a perfectly balanced potting compost while the fruits of these backyard plant propagations were traded from gardener to gardener.

The cottage garden remained a productive unit, where homegrown fruit and vegetables formed an important part of the family diet and plants like lemon balm, used to polish and scent furniture, were cultivated strictly for practical purposes. Nevertheless, by the early 1900s, the cottage gardener was growing petunias, pelargoniums, primulas and other flowers simply for their good looks. Architectural ornaments such as a rose temples, arches and hanging baskets, and practical features such as cold frame and espalier fruit (ideal for the small garden) were also being borrowed from the big house and incorporated into the cottage garden.

The simple, unpretentious nature of these little horticultural havens did not go unnoticed by those designers who were responsible for the great and grand gardens. Gertrude Jekyll wrote of cottage gardens: 'they have a simple and tender charm that one may look for in vain in gardens of greater pretension.' William Robinson was the greatest exponent of the natural garden and, although he spent most of his working life in England, he would have been influenced by his childhood days among the pretty gardens of County Down. He offered stern advice to his readers. 'Do not pay much attention to labelling; if a plant is not worth knowing it is not worth growing' was a favourite maxim. They were words of wisdom that had long been learned by the Irish cottage gardener.

In the present day, Irish gardens large and small are increasingly influenced by the old cottage-style gardens: the herbaceous border with its mixture of shrubs, perennials and annuals; a meadow-like lawn undersown with primroses, crocuses, snowdrops and grape hyacinths; and quiet corners of the garden naturally planted with shrubs or bulbs.

COUNTRY GARDENS

Country gardeners in Ireland today have a wealth of garden lore and a wide range of plants at their disposal, but they still have to contend with a variety of problems. When choosing suitable plants most gardeners have learned to be wary of any plantsman's promise that the tenderest exotic will survive and thrive in Ireland. The Irish climate varies from region to region. The relatively mild winters of southern Ireland allow the arbutus, or strawberry tree, with its soft, cinnamon-coloured trunk, to grow to a prodigious size and far larger than anywhere else in Europe. And yet the cool summers of the north rarely allow the walnut tree time to bear fruit in its shortened growing season. Mild County Meath to the east may be criss-crossed by verdant green hedgerows and prolific stands of beech, ash and sycamore, but away to the west in Counties Galway and Mayo, where dry stone walls dominate the landscape, the Irish

ABOVE

The strawberry tree, arbutus unedo, *with its distinctive peeling, red-brown bark survives and thrives under a benign Irish climate. But it earned its botanical name (*unedo – I eat one*) from the bland taste of the fruit.*

seaboard can throw furious gales inland that will trade sea salt for soil. Many gardeners still remember the January gales of 1974 that destroyed numerous old trees in areas as far inland as County Kildare.

Soil conditions also vary. They range from the stiff yellow clays of Tipperary, one of several counties that lay claim to possessing the best soil in Ireland, to the thick, peaty soils that border the Bog of Allen in Counties Offaly and Kildare. These soils hold their moisture, while some of the fast-draining, sandier soils will contribute to a local drought that, as some countrymen put it, can quickly send a tender plant to its tea. The best of the growing grounds are those that have been worked by generations of cottage gardeners; trial diggings on an old plot of land often reveal the darker, humus-rich sites where the vegetable plot or flower borders once stood. Virgin soils, such as those on former farmland, have had to be pre-

pared with winter applications of well-rotted manure or the products of the compost heap, rather than artificial fertilizers, to give them a good growing heart. (Regular applications of peat would help, but with the Irish peatlands disappearing at a profligate pace, the use of horticultural peat has become a matter of personal conscience.) Light, sandy soils can be improved immeasurably within a year of treatment while heavy, clay soils can take two, three or even four years to become workable.

In the old linen valleys of the north many new gardens have

BELOW

*B*y the late nineteenth century, garden designers had begun to appreciate the tender charms of the cottage garden with its apparently casual mix of flowers, fruits and vegetables. Such arrangements were soon to be adopted in what Gertrude Jekyll called 'gardens of greater pretension'.

been established on land once devoted to northern Ireland's most famous industry and several lily-filled pools and ponds have been created from the old reservoirs used to power the scutch mills where the flax for linen used to be prepared. Others gardens still struggle to overcome their industrial past and the abandoned rubble and buried masonry of a long-lost building can leave a lime-rich soil that many plants will not tolerate. Once again the solution is to sweeten the soil with liberal applications of humus in the form of well-rotted manure and garden compost.

A network of paths is the starting point for any new country garden. Traditionally a wandering affair of cinders and grit which wove its purposeful way between the flowers and veg-

etables to the orchard beyond, the meandering path has the distinct advantage of making a narrow garden appear wider than it actually is. As well as providing a dry-weather route through the greenery, garden paths serve as a natural divider between the different elements of the garden, for example, separating off a pond, a herb garden, a shrubbery and a vegetable patch. While central-heating systems have deprived the cottage path of its traditional supply of clinker, more permanent paths have been created by covering the ground with black polythene and laying gravel or a herringbone pattern of old bricks over the top. Liscannor flagstones and Scrabo stone have also been taken out of the old house undergoing renovation and, settled in a bed of sand, used to make a hopscotch

ABOVE

A distinctive garden within a garden, these stone troughs, planted with alpines, provide detail and colour early on in the gardening year.

LEFT

Hinting at the horticultural secrets that lie beyond, a stone-flagged path meanders between the borders of a cottage garden.

pattern of stepping stones through the garden. Alternatively these attractive old stones have been used as a natural substitute for concrete paving slabs on a terrace or sun-trapped courtyard where a host of creeping plants such as saxifrages, self-seeding aubrietias or, for their scent, thyme and lemon balm have been planted between the pavement crevices.

The Irish country garden drew its shape and form not only from the skeletal framework of its paths, but also from its banks and boundaries. Whole books have been devoted to the stone walls of Ireland, which grace many of the westerly country gardens with their silvery white sides, their patina of orange and green lichens and their house guests such as valerian and stonecrop. Stone walls, which provide an attractive background for foliage and flowering plants, have been constructed in loose rubble or neatly built in plain or herringbone pattern. In sheltered sites pockets of soil set in the wall have allowed plants such as pinks, wall flowers or, in shady conditions, ferns to colonize, while the base of the wall will always protect late-flowering plants well into the autumn. Banks of mounded peat lack the permanence of a stone wall, but they have been used to transform an alkaline-rich soil at their feet and turn it into a sheltered, humus-rich planting space for acid-loving rhododendrons and azaleas.

In exposed and coastline gardens a shelter belt or natural windbreak was almost obligatory and in extreme situations gardeners have had to content themselves with a low-level rock

LEFT
A small pond with lilies in the foreground and hostas in the background stands in a walled garden at Annes Grove in southern Ireland. A supremely romantic garden, it was laid out largely in the Robinsonian style.

or alpine garden until the shelter belt was at least waist high. Yet, once in place, a windbreak in the warm south-west is capable of protecting delicate, southern hemisphere species such as tree ferns, the tender and aromatic camphor tree (*Cinnamomum camphora*) or a perfumed stand of Californian tree poppies (*Romneya coulteri*). Trees and shrubs with variegation in their foliage have always provided an agreeable foil to the lush green of the Irish sward. Natural windbreaks have been planted from a colourful mix of prunus, hoheria, maple and conifer; the formal greenery of clipped yew (with its deep green backdrop so suited to the display of an urn or statue); or a traditional woodland mix of oak, sycamore and ash.

While England has its oak and Canada its maple, Ireland has no symbolic, national tree. The ash or *fuinseog* could be regarded as a leading candidate, since it was always prized as much for its good looks as it was for its firewood and timber. Ash was the traditional wood for the handles of pitchforks, spades and hurley sticks (used in this dangerously fast, hockey-like game). The ash is also a distant member of the olive family and, like the olive branch, the ash branch would be a significant symbol in the new Ireland.

One group of trees that have made a slow comeback are Ireland's old fruit trees. The march of the seasons used to be marked by the apple harvest and an orchard full of varieties like 'Irish Peach', 'Kerry Pippin', 'Ard Cairn Russet' and 'Ecklinville Seedling' would fill the fruit bowl with fresh fruit from the beginning of August through to the fading days of April. The two-hundred-year-old 'Irish Peach' which, despite its name, was a firm and juicy apple, ready for the table by early August, and the equally ancient 'Ross Nonpareil', which could be eaten through the Christmas period, were among some eighty Irish varieties. While many of these have been lost, some Irish fruit growers are cultivating stocks for the return of these traditional fruit trees.

When it came to choosing flowering plants, Irish gardeners have long accepted William Robinson's recommendation of 'the placing of perfectly hardy exotic plants in places where

'a gay or even a shabby garden – it is a rest to the mind and at all times a relief'

they will take care of themselves'. Old-fashioned plants like broom, catmint, feverfew, hollyhocks and roses, and old varieties like the double white primrose, the viola 'Irish Molly' or the shrub rose 'William Lobb', have traditionally had as sound a constitution as the country gardeners who used to grow them. These days, however, they are more likely to share their growing space with forget-me-nots from the Chatham Islands (*Myosotidium hortensia*), mountain daisies from New Zealand (*Celmisia*) and fuchsias from South America (*Fuchsia magellanica*), now well established throughout the west as a roadside hedge plant, and fiery azaleas underplanted with clutches of cyclamen and autumn crocus (*Colchicum autumnale*).

There was always a passion in Irish gardening circles for recreating other natural habitats, from bog gardens and water margins, to woodland glades, alpine banks and wildflower meadows. The traditional Irish bog was pretty enough with its bog pimpernel, asphodel and bogbean, but in a garden setting contemporary bog gardens can support other plants such as the feathery astilbe, skunk cabbage, hostas and candelabra primula.

The Irish gardener had a great fondness for garden architecture and ornaments, be it a fine set of entrance gates or a humble old kettle filled with a few geraniums and stood on an outside windowsill. Old stone troughs, their sides worn down from being used as a sharpening stone for the scythe, elaborate shrines, follies and grottoes, flower-filled urns and tubs, seats, benches and arbours, water pumps, sundials, barrels and busts have all found some secret corner of the Irish garden.

Trelliswork arches, which can support climbing shrubs such as roses and honeysuckle, were often used to create a scent-filled passage from the front garden to the back or from the flower garden to the vegetable plot. The old habit of using local materials such as willow or hazel wands, woven and tied or wired into shape, is usually preferable to buying standard sections from the garden store (although these may be improved by being given a coat of garden paint and allowed to fade for a season or two).

A sentry-box seat, created from a broken boat, invites the gardener to pause and ponder on that essential element of Irish country style – a place where, in Yeats' words, 'the soul's at ease'.

The most important transition of all is between the house and the garden: in the flower-crowded gardens of the traditional Irish country home, it was usually a seamless one. The stable-style half door, invariably left open to let more light into the kitchen, led straight through the old porch, itself invaded by fronds of clematis or ivy. This in turn opened directly out into the garden and family tasks such as carding a bit of wool or repairing a boot sole were often carried out, half-in or half-out of the porch, depending on the weather.

Conservatories have been used to serve as a place of passage between the house and garden for over a century, although many of the modern, store-bought conservatories, built to standard designs, make a less than sympathetic con-

tribution to the look of either the house or its garden. One solution, sometimes adopted by the Irish family returning to the home country from America or Australia, has been to construct a 'deck' or sheltered terrace on the sunny side of the house.

Places like these provide the ideal opportunity to relax and reflect, perhaps with a twinge of guilt, on the words of William Robinson: 'The aim of the gardener should be never to rest till the garden is a reflex of Nature in her fairest moods.'

BIBLIOGRAPHY

de Breffny, Brian and ffolliott, Rosemary, *The Houses of Ireland*, London, Thames & Hudson, 1975.

Jackson, Professor John A., *Irish Cottages*, Bray, County Wicklow, Real Ireland Design, 1993.

Keane, Molly, *Full House*, London, Virago, 1993.

———, *Good Behaviour*, London, André Deutsch, 1981.

Kinmonth, Claudia, *Irish Country Furniture 1700–1950*, London, Yale University Press, 1993.

Reid, Richard, *The Shell Book of Cottages*, London, Michael Joseph, 1997.

Sharkey, Olive, *Common Knowledge*, Melbourne, McPhee Gribble, 1988.

Shaw, George Bernard, *Man and Superman*, London, Penguin, 1988.

Shaw-Smith, David, *Ireland's Traditional Crafts*, London, Thames & Hudson, 1984.

Synge, J. M., *The Aran Islands*, Oxford, Oxford University Press, 1979.

Yeats, W. B., *Collected Poems*, London, Vintage, 1992.